ALLEN COUNTY PUBLIC LIBRARY

FORT WAYNE, INDIANA 46802

You may return this book to any agency, branch,
or bookmobile of the Allen County Public Library.

Development Administration and U.S. Foreign Aid Policy

Studies in Development Management

Series Editor: *Louis A. Picard*
National Association of Schools of
Public Affairs and Administration and
the University of Nebraska at Lincoln

A series of books prepared by
The National Association of Schools
of Public Affairs and Administration
and
The Development Program Management Center of
The United States Department of Agriculture,
sponsored by
The Bureau for Science and Technology of
The United States Agency for International Development

Development Administration and U.S. Foreign Aid Policy

Dennis A. Rondinelli

Lynne Rienner Publishers • Boulder & London

Published in the United States of America in 1987 by
Lynne Rienner Publishers, Inc.
948 North Street, Boulder, Colorado 80302

Library of Congress Cataloging-in-Publication Data

Rondinelli, Dennis A.
   Development administration and U.S. foreign
aid policy.

   (Studies in development management County Public Library
   Bibliography: p.
   Includes index.   Ft. Wayne, Indiana
   1. Economic development projects—
Developing countries—Management.   2. Economic
assistance, American—Developing countries.
I. Title. II. Series.
HC59.72.E44R66   1987   338.9′0068   87-4555
ISBN 0-931477-97-2 (lib. bdg.)

Printed and bound in the United States of America

The paper used in this publication meets the
requirements of the American National Standard
for Permanence of Paper for Printed Library
Materials Z39.48-1984 ∞

Contents

Series Foreword

Webster defines management as "the judicious use of means to accomplish an end." Applying management concepts to economic and social development programs in the Third World is a complex and multifaceted task because the manager must deal with elusive goals, changing environments, and uncertain means, and because optimal directions for organizing donor programs to assist the management of Third World programs have been ambiguous. The comparatively new field of economic and social development management is challenged to create more useful intellectual resources for both developing country management and donor cooperators.

Specialists in the field—managers, analysts, consultants, educators, and trainers—have found that to trace the academic base of development management is to draw a broad and interdisciplinary framework. Members of the development fraternity continually call attention to the diversity of the subject areas that are critical to the judicious management of social and economic change.

The need to develop a better understanding of development program management both in theory and practice has prompted the preparation of the current NASPAA/DPMC series. The Rondinelli book, analyzing the development management work that has been funded over the past fifteen years by the Agency for International Development (AID), examines some of the major research contributions to the development management field. The White, Hage-Finsterbusch, and Kerrigan-Luke volumes synthesize, probe, and order the academic bases for practice aimed at strengthening development management. Their subjects—development program management, organizational change strategies for more effective program management, and management training strategies for promoting improved program management—are purposely inter-related. The focus is on development programs in the Third World.

These books order and organize complex subjects. They thereby invite collateral analytic work by specialists in related concentrations and with related perspectives. In particular, we seek stronger links with work by Third World specialists, for although the authors have sought a Third World perspective, they have relied heavily on literature available in the United States.

The fifth book in the series presents the development management writing of one person. The Performance Management Project has valued the work of David Korten, chiefly in Asia, throughout his close to five years of work under the Project. His writings growing out of this work have found a wide and appreciative audience among those concerned with management for greater development strength at the grass roots. The Performance Management Project and NASPAA are pleased to include a compendium of his writings in this series and to have the opportunity to emphasize this aspect of development management.

The impetus and subsequent funding for the research discussed in this series came from the Performance Management Project in the Office of Rural and Institutional Development of AID's Bureau for Science and Technology. The research should be useful to both practitioners and educators interested in international development and related fields. A major purpose of the books, from the funder's point of view, is to make more explicit the links between the assimilated knowledge and skills of the development management practitioner and the literature base that supports development practice. This required creative, developmental work. We are grateful to the authors for their considerable investment in time and thought that have brought these results.

The organizations that have implemented the Performance Management Project—the National Association of Schools of Public Affairs and Administration, the Development Program Management Center and its cooperator, the International Development Management Center of the University of Maryland—have for a number of years undertaken a variety of practical and analytical work with developing country organizations for improved management. The NASPAA/DPMC Studies in Development Management series reflects an interaction between the individual authors and the experienced practitioners associated with the two implementing organizations.

I would like to express my appreciation to an extraordinary group of people connected with the Performance Management Project who have contributed to this series. These books build on the work of many practitioners and academics who have been associated with the Performance Management Project over the past seven years. Particular thanks go to Wendell Schaeffer, Louise White, and Merlyn Kettering, Project coordinators for the management training, organizational change, and program management books respectively; to the series editor, Louis Picard; and to the editorial committee who, from its inception, provided this venture with important direction and analytic support strengthened by practical experience. They and I, in turn, are grateful to the specialists outside the Project who have contributed substantially through their critiques of the manuscripts. We want to make appreciative note of the understanding, leadership, and support that the books in this series have received from Kenneth L. Kornher, chief of the USAID division which is responsible for institutional development and management research. Christopher Russell, Jerry French, Eric Chetwynd, John O'Donnell, and Robert McClusky also have provided valuable agency support to this project's research activities.

> *Jeanne Foote North*
> Project Officer
> The Performance Management Project
> Office of Rural and Institutional Development
> Bureau for Science and Technology
> Agency for International Development

Acknowledgments

Many people contributed to the completion of this review of development administration in the U.S. foreign aid program, and I am grateful for their help and encouragement.

Kenneth Kornher of the U.S. Agency for International Development first suggested the study, and Rudi Klauss and Louis Picard, directors of the Technical Cooperation Project in the National Association of Schools of Public Affairs and Administration, under whose auspices it was carried out, provided essential logistical support and helpful recommendations.

I received detailed comments on early drafts from Marcus D. Ingle, Morris J. Solomon, and David C. Korten; reactions to parts of the manuscript from John M. Cohen and Milton J. Esman; and helpful materials from John D. Montgomery and William Siffin.

Although the U.S. Agency for International Development provided funding and support for this study, my opinions do not necessarily reflect the policies or views of AID, and I alone am responsible for interpretations and conclusions.

Dennis A. Rondinelli

1

Development Administration in U.S. Foreign Aid Programs

Born of a revolution in which foreign governments sent help that was strategically important in winning the country's independence, the United States has been generous throughout its history in returning aid to friendly governments in time of war, crisis, or disaster. For more than a century, the United States sent money and supplies abroad as military assistance. But beginning in the 1940s, with the initiation of the "Good Neighbor Policy" with Latin America, the United States embarked on a deliberate, albeit cautious, policy of providing financial and technical assistance for promoting economic and social progress in foreign countries.

A far-reaching experiment in foreign aid began in the wake of World War II. Through the Marshall Plan, which became the foundation for the American foreign assistance program, the United States helped European countries to recover from the widespread destruction of one of the most devastating human conflicts in history by making available resources to feed millions of their displaced people and to rebuild their productive economies. From the successful experience with the Marshall Plan, the American government extended aid to the poor countries of the world where pervasive poverty posed a serious threat to political and economic stability in the postwar era. From those cautious beginnings in the 1940s, foreign aid grew to become an important instrument of U.S. foreign policy. The Economic Cooperation Administration (ECA), which carried out the Marshall Plan in Europe, was succeeded in 1951 by the Mutual Security Agency (MSA), which extended assistance to Asia and South America. MSA was, in turn, replaced in 1953 by the Foreign Operations Administration (FOA) and, in 1955, by the International Cooperation Administration

1

(ICA) and the Development Loan Fund. These organizations not only channeled security assistance to U.S. allies and potential friends in the developing world, but offered poor countries help in increasing their food production, educating their citizens, and industrializing their economies. By 1961, the U.S. foreign assistance program had diversified into a wide range of social, economic, and humanitarian activities and was reorganized into the Agency for International Development (AID). AID was directed by Congress to help create conditions that would allow poor countries to emerge from poverty.

Since 1960, the United States has been the largest contributor to multilateral organizations such as the World Bank and the United Nations, which provide money and technical expertise to poor countries throughout the world. In addition, since 1970, the United States has provided on average more than $3 billion a year in official bilateral assistance directly to poor countries (Selim, 1983). Moreover, the food aid program, Public Law 480, enacted by Congress in 1954, sends U.S. surplus agricultural commodities to governments and voluntary organizations in developing countries to supplement food supplies and to overcome famine following natural or man-made disasters.

AID now provides financial and technical assistance to about eighty countries in Asia, Africa, Latin America, the Middle East, and the Caribbean. Through a staff in Washington, and through USAID missions working with American embassies in developing countries, AID contracts with private firms, universities, and voluntary and charitable organizations to assist governments and private organizations in developing nations.

Although it accounts for a relatively small portion of the national budget and a small percentage of the United States' gross national output, foreign aid has always been controversial. It is regularly condemned by its enemies as a "giveaway program to ungrateful recipients." It is praised by its friends as a humanitarian effort reflecting U.S. willingness to help less fortunate neighbors in time of need. Aid is also viewed skeptically by many foreign and U.S. scholars as a politically motivated program for satisfying the United States' own foreign policy interests. The foreign aid program has always held a politically precarious position; it lacks a strong domestic political constituency despite the fact that each year more than 60 percent of foreign aid expenditures purchase American goods and services.

The results of those expenditures—to promote agricultural development, to improve education, health, population planning, and to support a wide variety of social, economic and technical activities— have been equally controversial. Even its critics recognize, however, that the U.S. foreign assistance program "over the years has developed from a temporary postwar measure into an extremely sophisticated and permanent instrument of U.S. foreign policy" (Abbott, 1973).

How much and how directly the U.S. foreign aid program has contributed to economic and social progress in poor countries remain controversial questions. But one of the most important lessons from the U.S. experience with foreign aid is that success in promoting economic and social progress not only depends on the ability of developing countries to define appropriate macroeconomic policies and to mobilize financial, human, and technological resources, it also depends heavily on their ability to manage those resources effectively. The impact of development assistance projects and programs is weakened substantially if foreign aid is mismanaged by organizations in either donor or recipient countries.

Thus, for more than thirty years, AID has been providing technical and financial assistance to developing countries to improve their administrative and managerial capabilities and to strengthen institutions that are responsible for implementing AID-funded development projects and programs. Since the beginning of the U.S. foreign aid program, institutional development has been an integral part and a primary instrument of aid. Indeed, in recent years both the problems of and emphasis on improving development administration have increased. More than 25 percent of all AID field projects now aim wholly or in part to improve the managerial performance of public and private institutions in developing countries. Hundreds of millions of dollars have been obligated by AID for projects of applied research on institutional development, project management, and development administration, for technical assistance to government agencies and private organizations to improve their management performance, and for training thousands of officials from developing nations in public administration and management in their own countries and in the United States. Governments in developing countries have also been struggling with the problems of managing foreign assistance and the development programs that that assistance is intended to support.

Despite the fact that the U.S. foreign aid program has devoted a large portion of its financial, administrative, and technical resources to improving organizational and management capacities in developing countries, administrative problems still undermine the capacity of AID and of public and private organizations in developing countries to implement development programs and projects effectively. For these reasons, the question of how to improve development administration is now receiving greater attention by most international assistance organizations and by many governments in developing countries. AID's strategic plan, *Blueprint for Development* (1985: 17), sees institutional development as a key to promoting sustainable economic growth and social progress in poor countries. It points out that "training to help build an indigenous analytical capacity to conceive, plan, and implement development strategies and programs is a very important component of institution building. The principal objectives of these efforts is to develop human resources and use them effectively in sustainable institutions."

The impact of these activities remains uncertain. Few systematic evaluations have been made of the results of these investments on administrative performance in developing countries, and observers of the approaches that AID has used over the years disagree on their effectiveness. Some argue that, in many developing countries, public administration is more effective and efficient than in the past and better than it would have been in the absence of aid. Others contend that some of the approaches to institutional development and management improvement used by AID have either had no impact or have exacerbated administrative problems.

Because of its importance in the U.S. foreign aid program, experience with development administration deserves more careful attention. This book examines the role of and approaches to development administration in U.S. foreign aid since the early 1950s. It does not provide answers to the controversial questions about how and to what extent U.S. foreign aid has contributed to economic and social progress in poor countries. Nor does it resolve the issue of whether the activities of AID and its predecessors have significantly strengthened the administrative and institutional capacity of organizations in poor countries to pursue economic growth and social progress more independently and efficiently. Instead, this book sets out the framework for understanding better what AID has been trying to accomplish in development administration, and how. Only after we understand better what AID has been trying to do can a larger community of scholars and practitioners of American foreign assistance hope to tackle the infinitely more complex task of assessing its effectiveness.

Importance of Development Administration in the U.S. Foreign Aid Program

Expanding the capacity of public and private organizations in developing countries to conceive, plan, and carry out development programs and projects has always been an important goal of U.S. foreign assistance, although its importance has often gone unrecognized by many of those professionals engaged in international development—especially by technical experts who specialize in one aspect of the development process. Usually its priority as an objective has been displaced by immediate political or military crises that focused attention on other goals. But it is widely recognized in American foreign aid doctrine that if economic and social progress is to be made and sustained, public and private organizations in developing nations must have the capacity to carry out their own development programs. Helping governments and private organizations in developing countries to create the managerial and institutional capacity to formulate and implement their own development strategies has been the explicit aim of U.S. foreign aid policy since the time of the Marshall Plan. Secretary of State George C. Marshall, in announcing the aid plan for Europe that would later bear his name, declared in 1947 that "it would be neither fitting nor efficacious for this government to undertake to draw up unilaterally a program designed to place Europe on its feet economically. This is the business of Europeans."

A strong consensus has evolved in the U.S. foreign aid program since 1947 that development assistance alone will have little impact on bringing about greater economic self-sufficiency and social progress unless public and private organizations in developing countries take a stronger role in planning and managing their own development. There is, however, an equally strong consensus that states that weaknesses in administrative capacity in developing countries create serious obstacles to faster economic and social progress and limit the effectiveness of U.S. foreign aid in promoting development.

The magnitude and pervasiveness of managerial and organizational problems in developing countries can be seen clearly by examining AID's internal evaluations. The USAID mission in Costa Rica, for example, has complained of "public sector inefficiency affecting nearly all of our programs" (1980a: 46). The USAID mission in Kenya has reported that "the insufficient quantity and inadequate quality of trained personnel and appropriate public and private sector institutions limit the formulation and hamper the implementation of necessary development programs, resulting in a suboptimal use of resources" (1980: 10). In Bangladesh, the USAID staff has observed that the government's "management systems and procedures are exceedingly cumbersome and hamper the expeditious release of funds, the recruitment and assignment of qualified personnel and internal agency realignments. There appears to be little communication, coordination or cooperation among ministries and agencies" (1980b:27).

Even in countries such as the Philippines, where government officials are well-trained, severe managerial and organizational problems continue to limit their ability to use foreign aid, to mobilize domestic resources, and to plan and manage development projects and programs effectively. The USAID mission in the Philippines contends that "in addition to the limitations on absorbing a much higher level of resources, there exist a number of institutional constraints to more effective use of resources that are received" (1980c: 36-37). The USAID staff points out that "the proliferation of implementing agencies, which results in rivalries, duplication of effort, and added costs, tends to handicap program implementation, especially in the absence of adequate management, monitoring and evaluation systems to cope with the added coordination requirements." Administrative capacity remains uneven among Philippine government institutions and this adversely affects the rate and effectiveness of implementation, especially in the health, education, population planning, and natural resource sectors. "Overly centralized decision making and administrative control severely limit the effectiveness of government programs," the mission's analysts note, and they inhibit the participation of local and regional governments in development planning and project implementation.

It has become clear over the past decade that bureaucracies in much of the Third World have limited capacity to plan and implement development projects effectively. A study by the Sudan's Management Development and Productivity Center, for example, concludes that development planning in the country is a confusing process in which the plans and programs of various agencies and ministries are often inconsistent or conflicting. Coordination and integration of plans among government agencies and public corporations are weak, and nowhere in the government structure is careful analysis done of policy alternatives. The ability of public organizations to implement plans and projects is equally weak. Most public organizations have long chains of command; managers have large spans of control that weaken their capacity to supervise subordinates; and there is often little relationship between these organizations' activities and their formal objectives and missions. Both government offices and public corporations are overstaffed and inefficient. High levels of personnel turnover in some organizations create instability, while in others middle- and lower-level managers can neither be fired nor disciplined effectively. Leadership within government organizations is weak, and public managers are given few incentives to perform their duties creatively or responsively (Weaver, 1979).

Similar deficiencies were seen in an assessment of Egyptian administration. Ayubi (1982: 295) concluded that:

> In general, the public bureaucracy is extremely large and complex. It is top-heavy, loosely coordinated, and very inactive at the lower levels. Overlapping and duplication are also widespread, and a large gap exists between formal and informal arrangements, while the excessive frequency of changes in laws, structures and leadership makes "organizational instability" a real problem. For example, the average period of tenure for an Egyptian minister is a year and a half, barely sufficient to enable him to familiarize himself with the tasks of the post.
>
> Administrative performance is so riddled with a number of related pathologies, such as the "idolization" of papers and documents, signatures and seals, routine and red tape, and the complexities and repetitiveness of a large number of formalities and procedures, all of which inevitably lead to bottlenecks and delays. Serious carelessness and negligence are also among the most dangerous of Egyptian bureaupathologies, recognized by a large number of experts, critics and politicians, as is the rapidly growing phenomenon of corruption in all shapes and forms.

Moreover, government agencies in most African countries have little ability to provide services effectively to peripheral regions or rural areas. Local administrative units have little authority, few skilled personnel, and inadequate financial resources to serve their constituencies or to implement development projects (Rondinelli, 1981, 1982; Cheema and Rondinelli, 1983). In Kenya, for example, administrative capacity to carry out the central government's development policies at the local level is quite constrained. Trapman (1974: 34) notes that the inability of central ministries to coordinate with each other leads to ambiguities in decisions in Nairobi and confusion in the provinces and districts. Often, he observes, "decisions have been made in isolation by heads of technical divisions and circulated as directives to the provincial offices without consultation either of the planners or of the field staff themselves." Either field staff attempt to apply irrelevant or inappropriate policies at the local level, or ignore the directives entirely.

In many African governments the entire administrative system "has a characteristic weakness in managing large-scale or complex activities beyond the capacity of one top executive to control directly," resulting in management by reaction to daily crises (Moris, 1977: 90). There is little capacity within government to guide or direct development projects toward larger goals.

The Impact of Administrative Problems on Foreign Aid

There has been a growing awareness in international assistance organizations that the most carefully planned and systematically
analyzed foreign aid projects are worthless unless they can be implemented effectively (World Bank, 1983). After examining a large
number of AID projects, the U.S. General Accounting Office, which
monitors and evaluates the agency's performance, recently reported
to Congress that "the management and effectiveness of AID projects
in health care, water development, agricultural assistance, as well as
projects to strengthen governmental institutions, ultimately depend
upon the abilility of host countries to absorb U.S. aid and implement
the projects." GAO officials argued that without this implementation
capacity "the results are either large obligations of unspent assistance funds or expenditure of funds for projects with limited life after
U.S. assistance is terminated" (Conahan, 1983: 341).

These findings were confirmed by AID's inspector general, who
testified before Congress that "we find in our reviews continuing implementation problems arising often, in my judgment, from some of
the practical weaknesses of the host country implementation capacity." He argued that the inspector general's reviews of AID-funded activities "have shown delayed projects, increased costs flowing from
these delays, frequent poor logistical support by host governments, a
general lack of audits of contract and grant costs by the host governments, procurement inefficiencies in the acquisition of both goods and
services, and administrative difficulties on the part of host governments in executing bid procedures, preparing contracts, and administering contracts" (Beckington, 1983: 372).

In a special study of West African countries, the inspector general
found "project after project undergoing serious delays and shortfalls
in reaching planned objectives. Host countries were experiencing
grave difficulties in executing many of the projects. Lack of host country funds, trained personnel, delayed procurements, overoptimistic
assessments of host country capabilities were contributing conditions." As a result, the inspector general questioned the viability of
many of these AID projects once U.S. financial and technical support
ended. Because of the low levels of management capacity in many developing countries, the inspector general concluded, "the AID investment of many millions of dollars could have been placed at serious
risk" (Beckington, 1983: 372).

Moreover, the General Accounting Office's review of AID's Sahel
Development Program found that, despite the fact that international
donors have spent more than $13 billion in this part of Africa over the

past ten years, most of the countries are no better off economically. The GAO recognized that the lack of progress was due to many economic, political, and physical problems in the area, but noted that a major problem contributing to slow rates of economic growth in the Sahel "is the weak capabilities of the Sahelian governments to plan and manage economic development and to coordinate donor activities" (USGAO, 1985).

AID has learned that expanding organizational capacity and management skills within developing countries is a prerequisite to eliciting the participation needed to ensure that governments are responding effectively to people's economic and social needs. "The development experience of the past two decades indicates that the impact and sustainability of public sector investments can be significantly improved if local citizens assume a role in needs assessment, project design and implementation," AID's strategic plan emphasizes. "Too often governmental organizations and programs are out of touch with the reality of development needs, and the problems and perspectives of low income groups. Local participation (in both urban and rural areas) is essential in adapting development priorities, designs and implementation strategies to particular contexts, and in communicating to planners local needs, constraints, and priorities." Participation is easier when nongovernmental organizations, as well as public agencies and private enterprises, have strong management skills and abilities.

Administrative Problems Within AID

To the extent that improving development administration involves close interaction between organizations in developing countries that are responsible for implementing foreign aid projects and donor organizations that provide financial and technical assistance, the ability of aid agencies to manage their own activities strongly influences the performance of host country governments and the outcome of development projects. AID's procedures for project planning, design and implementation, as will be seen later, directly affect the performance of organizations that manage projects in developing countries. They create an environment within which project and program managers in developing countries must operate, and often the procedures adopted by AID are prescribed as efficient management procedures for organizations in developing countries.

For nearly three decades, increasing evidence has been indicating that many of the problems with the implementation of foreign aid projects in developing countries come from ineffective management within AID. The agency's inspector general considers management to be the crucial variable influencing the outcome of foreign assistance projects and has recently concluded that "the management and administration of the foreign aid program pose severe challenges to managers and administrators at all levels of the AID organization" (Beckington, 1983: 369). Officials of the General Accounting Office concur, pointing out that "we have made quite a few recommendations on ways AID could improve its [own] program planning, project implementation and monitoring and evaluation. We have seen recent progress toward improved project planning and implementation, but quite frankly we believe much needs to be done" (Conahan, 1983: 338).

The inspector general argues that, despite the fact that many of these administrative problems have been reported repeatedly, AID's own management procedures are still weak. He has pointed out that cash management in many AID projects is inept or inadequate; monitoring and supervision of contractor performance are weak; procurement systems are inefficient; and commodity delivery systems are unreliable (USAID, 1983a). Thus the agency's problems exacerbate those of developing country governments in managing aid projects effectively.

Criticisms are made frequently of AID's project planning and programming and management cycle for being too rigid, overly controlled, and ineffective. Many projects take two to three years to be identified, designed, reviewed, and approved before assistance is ready to flow to a developing country. Although the complexity of the projects that AID supports may in some cases justify the time and resources invested in design, many of AID's own field staff believe that the procedures are not only cumbersome, but also ineffective (USGAO, 1983). Often, project design procedures and congressionally mandated administrative requirements become ends in themselves, complicating the process of development management and burdening organizations in developing countries. AID field staff must spend much of their time meeting these requirements or monitoring the compliance of host country governments, and little time can be devoted to interacting with intended beneficiaries or local project managers on substantive matters. In its review of AID projects in the Sahel, the General Accounting Office pointed out that the "provision of development assistance by the large number of donors and their administrative requirements places a considerable burden on recipient governments and strains their already weak administrative capabilities" (USGAO, 1985).

According to GAO studies, the large amount of time and resources spent by AID on project design has led to neither more effective project planning nor significant reductions in delays and cost overruns. Many projects end up being "judged on criteria unrealistic in terms of implementation and are approved as long as they are well articulated and presented in the proper form" (USGAO, 1983: 13). Because of the two- to three-year lag times between design and implementation, most projects are planned long before the host country project managers and technical assistance personnel have been selected. AID's inspector general points out that, for this reason, "we find the host country experiencing difficulties in carrying forward the project as it has agreed to do" (Beckington, 1983: 291).

Moreover, AID's inspector general contends that the agency's management and review procedures do not allow its administrators to discover implementation problems and to correct them quickly. "Responsibility for results is sometimes diffused organizationally between field and headquarters managers and over a succession of individuals. The result can be drift and indecision," the inspector general complains. "Clear warning signs of developing problems are not picked up and acted upon." As a result, projects fall behind schedule or are ineffectively implemented "without firm corrective action being taken at any level" (Beckington, 1983: 292).

One reason for the recurrence of development management problems is the strong internal pressures on AID staff to deal with current financial and administrative requirements. Some AID staff describe their jobs as a constant cycle of "money pushing" and "fire fighting." These pressures often wipe out the time to think, assess, and learn. There are strong pressures on AID field staff to expedite the approval of projects so that appropriations for each budget year can be obligated. Once a project is approved, USAID mission personnel must look toward the next set of projects rather than back to the lessons learned about those underway or completed. Thus little attention is given to recording the lessons of their own experience in order to improve their development management capacity and that of host country organizations (USGAO, 1982). GAO investigators have found that rather than being seen as useful means of helping their successors avoid mistakes or of avoiding those of their predecessors, the requirement of recording lessons learned is viewed by AID field staff as one to be complied with minimally or avoided altogether. This limits the capacity of AID to improve its own and host country government managerial practices and to strengthen development institutions in LDCs.

Thus, despite AID's success over the past three decades in sponsoring applied research on institutional development and management improvement, in training thousands of people from developing countries in administration and management, and in providing technical assistance for project and program management improvement to Third World governments, less developed nations—and AID itself— still face enormous problems with managing development activities efficiently and effectively.

A Historical Perspective on Development Administration in Foreign Aid Programs

After three decades of attempting to improve administrative capabilities in developing countries and to manage its own foreign assistance responsibilities more effectively, it is important to determine what AID has done and what has been learned from the experience.

Such a review is needed because AID's strategies and approaches to development have changed since the 1960s. Its mission has been redirected and its activities have been refocused several times. The rapid growth in knowledge about development administration and aid management in recent years has led to reassessments of the most effective approaches and interventions. Indeed, changes in thinking about development management have generated many new—and sometimes conflicting—strategies. Much of that knowledge and some of the strategies have resulted directly from applied research and pilot projects sponsored by AID. Thus a review of that experience and of the lessons learned from it can provide a "baseline" for identifying the kinds of applied research that must still be done on issues of development management, allow those providing training and technical assistance to distill important principles and guidelines for action, and consolidate knowledge that can be disseminated to institutions in developing countries.

This book seeks, first, to describe the evolution of AID's development management strategies over the past thirty years, especially those concerned with planning and implementing development projects and programs; second, to identify the approaches used by AID to improve development project and program management performance; third, to examine the reasons for the adoption of those strategies and approaches; fourth, to identify the assumptions or principles underlying them; and finally, to summarize important lessons learned from them and their implications for foreign aid policy in the future.

Because the concepts and definitions of development administration have changed over time, no single definition of the term is used here. Generally, the term "development administration" is used interchangeably with "development management" and "administrative development." It is also used to refer to three sets of activities within the U.S. foreign aid program: first, activities aimed at expanding the capacity of governments and private organizations in developing countries to conceive, plan, and implement economic and social projects funded with U.S. assistance; second, activities aimed at improving the effectiveness and efficiency of AID-funded and contractor-run development projects in developing countries; and third, activities aimed at improving AID's own internal operations. As will be seen, all three sets of activities are related to each other in the implementation of the foreign aid program.

A book such as this could be organized in many ways, but this one offers a chronological and historical perspective on AID's experience. Such a framework is useful for a number of reasons: first, the strategies and approaches used by AID have changed over time, and the evolution of thinking underlying those changes can only be seen clearly in historical perspective; second, a historical perspective shows that the changes were not merely random or arbitrary fads. Most of the changes in AID strategies for improving development administration resulted from the lessons learned from previous successes and failures. In some cases, they evolved from dissatisfaction within the agency, or from its constituencies, with previous approaches to development administration; in other cases, they were brought about by evidence that interventions seemed to be effective in promoting change. In still others, the new knowledge that came from AID's own evaluations or from the applied research that it had sponsored was the source of change. It is important to keep in mind that all international assistance agencies have, over the past three decades, been engaged essentially in a "learning process."

Third, a chronological examination indicates that AID's activities in improving development administration have been strongly shaped and directed by changes in U.S. foreign policy. Changes in agency priorities have largely determined how development administration interventions could be defined in AID, the sectors and problems to which they could be addressed, the kinds of requests that were made for assistance by USAID missions, and the types of projects that AID could reasonably expect to have approved and funded.

Fourth, the historical examination of changes in AID's development administration activities illustrates, implicitly at least, that they were shaped as well by a large number of constituencies. The political and technical priorities of the agency are influenced by Congress, the White House, the governments to which aid is provided, the State Department's interpretation of U.S. foreign policy, and to some degree by the fact that economic and military assistance are often closely linked. Moreover, technical offices within AID are influenced directly or indirectly by the thinking and methods of their contractors and consultants, by academic research and the changing theories of economic and social development that result from it, by the interaction between USAID mission staff and counterpart officials in developing countries, and by the experience and perspectives of the individual staff members working in those offices. Many of these influences are seen clearly in the examination of AID experience that follows.

The contention that AID's strategies to improve development management have been largely evolutionary and based on a long process of learning does not imply that there has always been agreement within the agency on those strategies or on the lessons that have been learned from previous experience. Nor does it imply that the lessons have always been applied within the agency. AID staff, contractors, consultants, mission personnel, and counterparts in developing countries often have very different perspectives on management needs and on the value of different techniques of intervention and training.

The fields of development administration and management theory are replete with contending schools of thought, and the thinking within AID has reflected that diversity. Crawley (1965: 169) pointed out nearly two decades ago that debates in AID over proper management approaches included arguments over the following schools of theory:

1. *The management process school.* Management is the process through which people who operate in organized groups get things done. Therefore, to build a theory of management it is first necessary to analyze the process, establish a conceptual framework and try to identify the principles behind the process.

2. *The empirical school.* Management is conceived as a study of experience, sometimes with the intent to draw generalizations but often only as a means of transferring this experience to practitioners and students.

3. *The human behavior school.* Since managing involves getting things done with and through people, the study of management must be centered on interpersonal relations.

4. *The social system school.* Management is in reality a kind of social system—that is, a system of cultural interrelationships which is sometimes limited to formal organizations but may encompass any kind of system of human relationships.

5. *The decision theory school.* This approach concentrates on rational approaches to decision-making, emphasizing the selection of a course of action or of an idea from various possible alternatives.

6. *The mathematical school.* Management is perceived as a kind of system of mathematical models and processes based on the assumption that management or decision-making is a logical process which can be expressed and understood in terms of mathematical symbols and relationships.

Differences remain between those who believe that management is a science and those who are convinced that it is an art.

The tensions are often exacerbated by the fact that AID is a complex organization in which many objectives are pursued simultaneously. Many of AID's career staff see their primary objective as supporting U.S. foreign policy. Others consider it the primary objective of foreign assistance to help the poor in developing countries to become more independent and self-sufficient. In theory, AID considers the two objectives to be consistent; in practice, they often are not.

In the chapters that follow, the strategies of development administration and management that have been used in AID are traced historically. Chapter 2 describes the approaches to development administration that emerged during the 1950s and 1960s when the "Point Four" technology transfer approaches were dominant and when AID adopted administrative reform and institution-building approaches. Chapter 3 examines AID experience in the early 1970s when the agency concentrated on sectoral systems and internal project management improvement. Chapter 4 explores the period from the mid- to late 1970s when the "New Directions" mandate refocused AID's concern on "people-centered" approaches to designing and managing programs and projects to reach the "poor majority." AID's experience in the early 1980s with organizational development strategies, decentralization, and learning processes is examined in Chapter 5. Chapter 6 reviews the results of an assessment of the role of management in effectively implementing AID projects in Africa. The assessment provides an empirical perspective on the validity of the theoretical conclusions of AID's research on development administration. The last chapter explores the prospects for improving development administration through the U.S. foreign aid program, and the implications for AID strategies in the future.

2

Development Administration as
Technology Transfer

U.S. technical assistance for development administration during the 1950s and early 1960s was heavily influenced by previous experience with foreign aid and by the prevailing concepts and theories of economic development. Prior to and during World War II, U.S. foreign aid went to allies primarily as military assistance. Immediately after the war, the U.S. contribution for emergency relief was channeled through the United Nations Relief and Rehabilitation Administration (UNRRA) and the International Bank for Reconstruction and Development. Modest amounts of bilateral aid were provided to European countries and to the Philippines for "government and relief in occupied areas" beginning in 1946, and more substantial amounts were provided directly to Greece and Turkey in 1947 as part of the Truman Doctrine to assist those countries in resisting Soviet subjugation.

Nearly all efforts to assist Western European countries were justified by the U.S. government's concern for preventing the spread of communism and Soviet influence. The Truman administration's dissatisfaction with UNRRA's distribution of assistance to Eastern European bloc countries and with the lack of U.S. control over its contributions to United Nations relief programs created the demand for bilateral aid. U.S. economic and military aid was given to Greece and Turkey to strengthen their ability to resist Soviet aggression, and Secretary of State George C. Marshall initiated a broad policy review of U.S. foreign aid in 1947 that led to proposals for a program of economic assistance for all of Western Europe. In his address at Harvard University in June 1947, Marshall announced a U.S. assistance policy that would provide "a cure rather than a mere palliative" to European economic problems resulting from the ravages of World War II (Arkes, 1972).

When the United States began seriously to provide assistance for economic development through the Marshall Plan in 1948, U.S. efforts were focused almost entirely on rebuilding the physical and industrial structure of those European countries that had attained high levels of productive capacity prior to World War II. Although Marshall proclaimed that "our policy is directed not against any country or doctrine, but against hunger, poverty, desperation and chaos," the underlying goal was clearly to strengthen the economies of European countries for security purposes and against the possibility of Soviet domination. The Economic Cooperation Administration (ECA) was created as a semiautonomous agency under the supervision of the Secretary of State to assist sixteen European countries to formulate long-range plans for restoring production and trade to prewar or higher levels. U.S. aid was aimed primarily at rehabilitating physical infrastructure and industrial plants, temporarily feeding large numbers of people whose sources of income had been destroyed during the war, and reestablishing the economies of industrial societies.

The principles of the Marshall Plan had a strong influence on the U.S. foreign aid program for more than a decade. Clearly, the Marshall Plan was seen by both the administration and Congress as a temporary instrument of U.S. foreign policy. The European Recovery Program (ERP) was defined as a joint effort based on self-help for a four-year period after which, if the program were successful, it would no longer be needed. The program encouraged cooperation between the United States and European countries. European governments were to share authority with the United States in deciding how U.S. aid would be used. ECA created overseas missions in the countries receiving aid so that U.S. representatives could participate in the planning and allocation of aid funds. In addition to strengthening the capacity of European countries to defend themselves, the ERP was seen as a means of promoting U.S. trade and business. Provisions were made in the legislation establishing the European Recovery Program for procurement of surplus U.S. agricultural and industrial goods, for the promotion of trade between the United States and the recovering European economies, and for assuring access of U.S. industries to scarce production materials (Arkes, 1972).

With the rehabilitation of European economies underway, U.S. foreign assistance was extended to poorer countries, and similar methods of technology transfer and infrastructure construction were used in an attempt to promote high levels of economic growth. In 1948, congressional interests supporting the governments of China and the

Republic of Korea pushed for an ECA program in Asia. Although the Truman administration explained that ECA rehabilitation programs were not necessarily applicable in those countries because of different economic and political circumstances, Congress initiated aid programs for China in 1948 and Korea in 1949. The fall of mainland China to the Communists in 1949, despite large amounts of U.S. military assistance to Kuomintang forces, led many in Congress and the State Department to believe that military aid to poor countries was not sufficient and that the only way to bolster their resistance to Communist aggression was through a combination of military and economic assistance (Wolf, 1960).

The belief that economic assistance was essential to supplement military support for poor countries was reflected in President Truman's inaugural address in January 1949. The fourth point in the policy agenda for his new administration called for "a bold new program for making the benefits of our scientific advances and industrial progress available for the improvement and growth of the underdeveloped areas." He requested from a reluctant Congress funds for technical assistance, capital investment, and private investment guarantees for developing nations, especially for those threatened by Communist insurrections or invasions—a program that was to become known as "Point Four."

U.S. fears of Communist aggression and the lessons of experience in China were to influence the State Department's approach to foreign aid until late into the 1960s. In 1950, Secretary of State Dean Acheson saw "the susceptibility of many countries in the Pacific area to subversion and penetration . . . that cannot be stopped by military means." He argued that the security of developing countries in Asia required assistance "to develop a soundness of administration of [the] new governments and to develop their resources and their skills so that they are not subject to penetration either through ignorance, or because they believe false promises or because there is real distress in their areas. If we can help that development," he insisted, "then we have brought about the best way that anyone knows of stopping this spread of communism" (Wolf, 1960).

With the fall of mainland China in 1949 and increasing hostilities in Korea, the administration requested the consolidation of scattered and sporadic aid programs. In 1950, Congress passed the Act for International Development, which declared the policy of the United States to be "to aid the efforts of the peoples of economically underdeveloped areas to develop their resources and improve their working and living conditions by encouraging the exchange of technical knowledge and skills and the flow of investment capital to countries which provide conditions under which such technical and capital can effectively and constructively contribute to raising the standards of living, creating new sources of wealth, increasing productivity and expanding purchasing power."

During the 1960s, officials in the U.S. foreign aid program believed that technical assistance could help develop the "soundness of administration" that Acheson had referred to, and that U.S. capital assistance and investment could help stimulate economic growth. Economic growth would raise the living standards of the population and create a stable political environment in which people would be less susceptible to subversion and better able to defend themselves against a Communist takeover.

Economic development was measured primarily by increases in gross national product (GNP). Gross national product, it was believed, could be increased most rapidly by raising the level of industrial output. Developing nations were urged to seek large amounts of foreign capital, to build on their comparative advantages in low-wage manufacturing or in raw materials exporting, and to apply capital-intensive technology in their production processes. Export-oriented or import substitution industries were usually favored. Agriculture would be modernized by the application of commercial fertilizers, modern machinery, and the technology used in Western countries. Strong emphasis was placed as well on political modernization and administrative reform to create conditions that development theorists thought were essential to promote rapid economic growth and social change.

The U.S. foreign aid program was imbued with a strong belief that poor countries could be developed quickly by accelerating their progress through the same stages of development that Western industrial countries had presumably gone through. It was widely assumed that developing countries would follow three stages of economic development that Rostow (1952) insisted had taken place in Western countries: first, a long period when the preconditions for economic "takeoff" are established; second, the takeoff period itself; and third, a long period when economic growth would be normal and automatic. According to the stage theory of economic growth, the preconditions for the takeoff would be established when the economic motives for growth began to converge with noneconomic motives. The preconditions included the spread of education, the emergence of an entrepreneurial group willing to mobilize savings and take risks in investment, the growth of commercial markets for agricultural products, rising demand for manufactured consumer goods, the creation or expansion of institutions for mobilizing capital, and the extension of transport and communications to serve commerce and industry.

When these conditions appeared, Rostow contended, additional stimuli would be needed to bring the economy to the takeoff stage. In this stage, the forces of economic development would become reinforcing and lead to higher rates of innovation and investment.New industries would expand rapidly, and the profits would be reinvested in new production capacity. Institutions for mobilizing capital would also expand significantly, new techniques would be applied in agriculture and industry that would increase their productivity, new possibilities for export and new import requirements would emerge, and the economy would exploit previously unused backlogs of natural resources and technology to reach still higher levels of production.

Although Rostow's stage theory of development was controversial, the major debates among economists concerned the best means of achieving the takeoff. Some argued that the best way of attaining high levels of economic growth was through heavy investment in industry or economic infrastructure as the "leading sector." Growth of the leading sector would spur and stimulate the economy and create "ripple effects" that would create demand for increased output in other sectors (Hirschman, 1959). Other economists argued that a "big push" was needed in all sectors at the same time to increase output and generate demand for industrial goods.

Most economists accepted Kuznets' (1966) theory that, although in the initial stages of economic growth the largest share of income would accrue to higher income groups, eventually through "trickle down" and ripple effects of economic growth the benefits would spread throughout the economy and the relative share of income of the poor would increase. The rising level of income would create greater demand for agricultural goods and the application of new technology would make agriculture more productive and less labor-intensive. Surplus agricultural labor would be absorbed in the expanding industrial sector (Lewis, 1955). As agricultural production increased, profits would be reinvested in more efficient technology, better seed varieties, irrigation, and other manufactured inputs that would generate higher yields with less labor and land. Rostow and others believed that the exploitation of land and natural resources would stimulate the growth of a self-sustaining industrial sector because the export of natural resources would generate for poor countries the capital needed to finance industrial expansion and to service foreign debt. After the economy reached the takeoff stage, the poor would begin to benefit and the growth cycle would continue to generate higher levels

of output, create incentives for diversification, and allow more technologically advanced industries to succeed low-wage industries and
natural resource exporting activities.

Thus the early period of U.S. foreign assistance was based on two
strongly prevailing paradigms: the economic growth model just described, and the political modernization model. Technical assistance
would help modernize both the economic and the political systems of
developing countries, and capital assistance would help developing
countries mobilize the funds needed for investment. Therefore, U.S.
economic aid was allocated primarily for projects in agriculture, industry, and transportation, although substantial amounts of money
were also provided for health, public administration, education, and
community development.

These two compatible paradigms of economic growth and political
modernization converged to form the intellectual basis for U.S.
foreign aid and justified technical assistance for development administration during the 1950s and 1960s. The major assumptions of these
models, as Esman (1980) points out, were that: (1) all societies could
modernize and grow economically in a sequence of historically veri-
fied stages that had occurred in Western nations over the previous two
centuries; (2) this modernization and growth could be accelerated in
poor countries through the transfer of resources and technologies
from industrialized nations; (3) the state, primarily through the central government, would be the principal instrument of promoting economic growth and of guiding modernization; (4) central governments,
through comprehensive and effective planning and management,
could guide or control the economic, social, and political forces
generating growth and modernization; (5) well-trained technical and
professional personnel in central government bureaucracies, using
modern administrative procedures and supported by benevolent and
development-oriented political leaders, would serve as the catalysts
for modernization and development; (6) leaders of developing countries, eager for growth and modernization, would sacrifice other
values and—with the help of Western advisors—would provide the
political and moral support necessary to achieve these goals; (7) the
transformation of underdeveloped societies from poverty would be
rapid and the benefits of growth would be widely shared; and (8) development would create the preconditions for political stability that
eventually would lead to democratic participation in economic and
political activities.

These principles shaped the approaches to foreign aid and development administration that were applied throughout the 1950s.

The Technology Transfer Approach

During the 1950s and 1960s, technical assistance in both leading economic sectors and in public administration took the form of what Esman and Montgomery (1969: 509) called the "Point Four Model." This consisted of transferring U.S. administrative technology and "know-how" to less developed countries, much in the same way that industrial and agricultural technology and economic know-how were transferred through the Marshall Plan. This approach assumed that successful methods, techniques, and ways of solving problems and delivering services in the United States or other economically advanced countries would prove equally successful in developing nations. Many of those involved in technical assistance in the early years of the foreign aid program believed that improving administrative capacities in developing countries was crucial to all other development activities. Brown (1964: 69-70) later quoted a health specialist providing technical assistance in one developing nation as saying that "the conduct of a DDT program . . . is 90 percent administration and 10 percent how to spray."

ECA and its successor, the International Cooperation Agency (ICA), as well as other international assistance agencies, spent large amounts of money on establishing institutes of public administration in developing countries, bringing people from developing nations to the United States to study public administration, and providing in-service training programs in developing countries. The United Nations, AID, and the Ford Foundation together spent more than $250 million during the 1950s alone on institution building and public administration training. AID helped establish institutes of public administration in many countries, including Brazil, Mexico, Peru, Ecuador, El Salvador, Korea, Pakistan, the Philippines, Thailand, and Vietnam. More than 7,000 people from developing countries were brought to the United States to study public administration under the auspices of international funding agencies during the 1950s (Paul, 1983: 19).

Much of the knowledge transferred abroad, and most of the training given in the United States, was steeped in conventional administrative theory. It emphasized, in the Weberian tradition, the creation of a politically neutral civil service in which modern methods of management, budgeting, personnel administration, contracting, procurement, supervision, and auditing would be applied. Underlying the transfer of Western tools of administration was a prevailing belief that unless the administrative and political systems of developing countries could be modernized there would be little chance of reaching the "takeoff" to economic growth. Indeed, Ilchman (1971) compared the prescriptions for administrative reform and the "takeoff into rational administration" to the various stages of Rostow's model for economic growth. Traditional administrative systems were characterized by centralization of decision making in a predominantly decentralized system of enforcement; orientation toward law and order, revenue collection, and a few major enterprises; slow and infrequent changes in procedures and methods of transacting affairs; and, failure to conceive of government in productivity terms. In traditional societies, the opportunities for government service were limited to notables and the elite, and ascriptive criteria dominated in the recruitment of officials. There was little occupational permanence or functional specialization in administrative institutions.

The preconditions for rationalizing the administrative system included the centralization of decision making and enforcement, the separation of public and private functions, the use of budgets as mechanisms of control, and the creation of a permanent group of government officials and civil servants. Preconditions would also include growing pressure for using skill and talent as the criteria for appointment to the civil service and the adoption of a system of well-defined, but limited, salaries for government officials. Other indicators of modernization included increasing functional specificity in organizations, the development and use of statistical services, the decline of religious influence on recruitment, and the emergence of the military as a transforming organization.

The takeoff into rational administration would come about as the result of recruiting and promoting government administrators by merit, the rise of a self-conscious administrative class, continued functionalization of ministries, expansion of statistical services, elaboration of the budget as a tool for control, an increasing concern for efficiency, and an increasing emphasis on government as producer of goods and services. Rationalization would also result from experimentation with new institutional forms such as boards, commissions, and inspectorates, and the emergence of the ministry of finance and the planning commission as transforming organizations.

Typical of the U.S. foreign aid program's public administration assistance during the 1950s and 1960s was a contract it gave in 1955 to Michigan State University to strengthen the National Institute of Administration (NIA) in Vietnam. The contract provided funds to place in Vietnam an advisory group "to make the National Institute of Administration an effective institution capable of developing the administrative skills and effectiveness of the Vietnamese Civil Service," as noted one participant in the project (Xuan, 1970: 373). "The long-range purpose was to improve the administrative performance of the government of Vietnam and thus contribute to its social and economic development." The Michigan State University Advisory Group (MSUG) provided assistance in what became rather typical activities for these types of projects: development of curricula and teaching methods, an in-service training program for government officials, a research program and reference library, training of the existing and potential new NIA staff, and development of case studies and training materials to be used in the NIA's training programs.

On the advice of the U.S. advisors, the school was moved from the old imperial capital of Dalat to Saigon. The MSUG revamped the curriculum of NIA to introduce more social science courses into what had been a legalistic orientation so that Vietnamese officials could become "generalist" administrators. The U.S. advisors attempted to expand the teaching method from one of lectures only to discussions and seminars requiring term papers and the analysis of case studies. The MSUG team wrote complete sets of lectures for new courses that were translated into Vietnamese, and chose texts and collateral readings for the courses. With the assistance of the MSUG, the NIA developed a library of more than 16,000 social science books, 1,000 United Nations documents, and 150 periodical subscriptions, nearly all in English.

Although the curriculum went through several revisions, courses were introduced in public administration, economics, finance, law, statistics, drafting of administrative documents, and accounting. Courses were also developed in civil service procedures, labor relations, economic planning, human relations, office management, budget practice, and organizational methods. The content of the courses was either adopted from U.S. textbooks or from lectures given in English by MSUG advisors in the NIA.

MSUG trained NIA staff primarily by sending them to the United States for four- to nine-month observation and study tours. Seventeen existing or potentially new staff were provided with Ph.D.-level training in the United States.

The cost of the project over a seven-year period included $5 million for MSUG salaries and operations in Vietnam, $5 million in local currency for its Vietnamese staff and field activities, and $15 million for equipment and materials, and totaled more than $25 million. At the peak of the project's activities, it had a staff of fifty-one Americans and 151 Vietnamese. Nearly all of the resources were spent on improving programs in public administration and in police administration.

Although both the U.S. Foreign Operations Administration and the NIA considered the project successful, a number of problems arose. Most of those trained in the United States and in Vietnam were from the country's political and social elite. Most of the materials developed or procured for the NIA were in English rather than in Vietnamese or French, the dominant languages spoken by Vietnamese government officials. Doctoral students were sent to the United States for long periods of time, were slow in completing their studies, and were sometimes reluctant to return to Vietnam after experiencing better living conditions in the United States. Some of those who did return did not want to work for NIA and chose positions in the government, leaving the institute chronically short of staff. With the overthrow of the Diem regime in 1963, the leadership of the NIA was changed and many of the staff left or were replaced. Moreover, the NIA was never able to meet the need for trained administrators in Vietnam; the annual output of NIA graduates was small compared to the number of officials who needed training in order to carry out their tasks effectively. Finally, a former staff member of NIA raised a basic philosophical problem. "Some have agreed that an increase in bureaucracy tends to inhibit rather then encourage development. In such a case the main function of NIA—training more and more civil servants for the government—might be considered as having a negative effect on development" (Xuan, 1970: 393).

In most of the foreign aid program's public administration assistance projects, it was assumed that the transfer of Western techniques to the developing world—what Siffin (1976) later called a "tool-oriented" approach—would improve administrative performance. It was assumed that administrative capacity for development could be expanded simply by adopting the approaches that had been successful in economically advanced countries without seriously examining the political conditions or administrative needs in developing nations. Strong emphasis was also placed on "administrative reform" to bring about organizational changes in government bureaucracies, which were often considered to be irrational, politically influenced, ineffective, and corrupt.

But the tool-oriented or technology transfer approach to development administration came under severe criticism during the 1960s. In a study prepared for AID, Esman and Montgomery (1969: 509) pointed out that:

> Much U.S. knowhow is ill-suited to the needs of many less developed countries. While Americans learned to economize on labor, these countries have labor surpluses and acute scarcity of capital. Many of our techniques, if they were to be useful, depend on other com-

plementary skills and organizations which are assumed in America, but do not exist in other countries. Western technology has also encountered unexpected cultural barriers. For example, it presupposed attitudes toward time, the manipulation of the physical world, and the proper relationships among men and between men and government which simply do not prevail in many societies. Many innovations which an U.S. considers purely technical were seen as threatening to men in other cultures. . . . Technological innovation sometimes brings drastic changes in the social, political and personal behavior of many individuals. In many instances, our overseas partners in technical cooperation accepted U.S. practices in a literal or formal way, but applied them with quite unexpected results.

Others noted that the administrative tools and concepts transferred to developing countries were not, in fact, merely neutral instruments for increasing administrative capacity. They were methods of administration that grew out of the U.S. political experience and Western democratic values. They placed strong emphasis on such concepts as separation of powers and specialization of functions within government, separation of politics and administration, and the belief that administration was a technical, nonpolitical activity. U.S. public administration theory was imbued with a hierarchical view of decision making and management. It emphasized decision making by rule of law and impartiality in the administration of laws. It assumed that merit and skill should be the basis for personnel selection and promotion in the civil service system. It also assumed the desirability of strong executive power, authority, and control in the administration of government activities. The major underlying assumption was that the transfer of Western administrative tools would lead to a high level of efficiency and effectiveness—the most highly valued goals of Western administrative theory—in developing nations (Siffin, 1976; Ingle, 1979).

The application of the Western techniques often produced unanticipated effects, or had no impact at all on improving administrative procedures in developing countries. In some cases, the techniques were detrimental to those societies to which they were transferred. Siffin (1976: 63) notes that the transfer of American administrative techniques and procedures "largely ignored the human side of administration and the real problems of incentives. It afforded no foundation for the study of policymaking and administrative politics. And it simply did not fit the realities of most of the developing countries of the world."

Indeed, the whole concept of technology transfer underlying the Point Four program came into question in the 1950s. Willard Thorp

(1951), one of the early planners of the European Recovery Program later pointed out that the most serious problems of technology transfer lay in the fact that "we are woefully ignorant of contemporary social and economic institutions in most other countries. It is clear that these other societies and cultures cannot and should not be made over in the U.S. image, but our accumulated social science knowledge has all too little to tell us about the possibilities and limitations of economic development in the underdeveloped countries."

Esman and Montgomery (1969: 514-515) later urged AID to abandon the transfer of U.S. public administration techniques as the primary means of providing technical assistance in development administration and, instead, to address more directly "the problems of fostering developmental change through technical cooperation." This alternative approach would:

1. Define projects in broad sectoral terms that link them directly to major systems of action
2. Encourage the use by host governments of mixtures of public, market, and voluntary instrumentalities as defined by specific local capabilities
3. Concentrate on experimental activities for which there are no readily available standard solutions, in which the United States and local participants can engage in solving important developmental problems through a cooperative learning process
4. Make full collegial use of local human resources in jointly directed experimental programming
5. Sustain our participation long enough to build indigenous institutions that represent real additions to the capacity of the host country to deal with increasingly complex problems
6. Make use of the most advanced management technologies in selected projects for pilot and demonstration purposes
7. Select activities as targets of opportunity on pragmatic judgments of their importance, the strength of domestic support, and the capacity of the United States to deliver assistance effectively
8. Make use of technical cooperation activities to improve the quality of civic life of those affected

Some of these recommendations were reflected in changes in AID's approaches to project and program management during the 1970s, others were ignored, and some were "rediscovered" by those assessing the impact of technical assistance in the early 1980s.

The Community Development Movement

Another means of promoting economic growth and political moderni-zation used extensively during the 1950s and 1960s was community development. This approach was adopted by ICA as a way to accelerate social change, inculcate the spirit of democracy, create conditions that would ensure political stability, and promote social welfare for the masses of the poor in developing nations. In many ways, the community development movement reflected all of the underlying assumptions of the Point Four approach. It fit Americans' image of local democracy. It made heavy use of methods developed to assist with agricultural and rural development during the New Deal and to assist the poor in American slums and ghettos during the previous half century. Moreover, it relied heavily on American urban and rural community development advisors and on agricultural and social services technicians who could use American goods and technology to promote local development abroad.

The movement was based on a set of concepts and procedures that had long been used to assist the poor in cities and rural areas of the United States. Community development, as it was practiced in the United States, has been described (Kramer and Specht, 1975: 6) as "the interactional processes of working with an action system which include identifying, recruiting, and working with members and developing organizational and interpersonal relations in formulating plans, developing strategies and mobilizing the resources necessary to effect action."

Community development followed a fairly standard pattern nearly everywhere it was practiced: (1) working with the residents of a community to identify their major problems and elicit their participation in programs designed to deal with them; (2) creating or strengthening social relationships among members of the community and building group cohesion so that they could pursue common action to overcome local problems; (3) identifying goals and actions to remedy or ameliorate community problems; (4) assisting individuals to assume positions of leadership for organizational development and local action; (5) developing organizational structures that allow community residents to build an effective constituency or coalition for taking action and pressing authorities for help and resources; (6) developing and extending linkages of communication and interaction with other groups and organizations that have resources or authority; (7) creating the capacity among local residents to plan, manage, and implement a program to deal with current problems and future changes; (8) developing mechanisms and arrangements for participation and coordination; and (9) increasing the organizational capacity of community residents to anticipate and adjust to social changes on a continuing basis (Brager and Specht, 1973). The individuals and organizations that promoted community development were "change agents" who facilitated the processes of local organizational development and resource mobilization.

In his retrospective assessment of the movement for AID, Holdcroft (1978: 10) correctly points out that the agency adopted the community development process because it was perceived to fit so well with the ideology underlying the Point Four approach to development assistance, and because it was seen from the Cold War perspective as an effective instrument for promoting political stability. AID defined community development as a program that "(a) involves people on a community basis in the solution of their common problems; (b) teaches and insists upon the use of democratic processes in the joint solution of community problems, and (c) activates or facilitates the transfer of technology to the people of a community for more effective solution of their common problems."

Beginning in the early 1950s, AID sent teams of technical assistance personnel, both to act as policy advisors and to assist with program design, to those countries where governments expressed an interest in establishing community development programs. Most of the programs were self-help efforts to assist villagers to establish small-scale health, education, sanitation, and social services, obtain agricultural extension services, and construct small-scale infrastructure, such as roads, bridges, dams, and irrigation ditches. AID also provided capital assistance for community development projects in some countries.

A Community Development Division was established in AID in 1954 to coordinate the agency's activities and to disseminate information about what had become, by the mid-1950s, a worldwide movement. Community development was supported not only by AID, but by the Ford Foundation and other voluntary organizations, several United Nations specialized agencies, and other bilateral donors. AID produced a periodical, The Community Development Review, which was distributed widely throughout the world until the early 1960s. AID also sponsored six international conferences—in Iran, Libya, Ceylon, Korea, and the United States—as forums for exchanging experience and disseminating information about community development.

Advocates of community development argued that the objective of economic and social modernization was to improve the lives of people in developing countries and that the movement was one of the most effective ways of doing so for the masses of the poor. They contended that the approach was also an economically sound form of national development because it mobilized underused labor and resources with minimum capital investment and extended the impact of scarce government specialists in health, education, social services, and agriculture through the coordinated efforts of community development agents. Furthermore, they argued that community development was the most effective way of promoting and guiding change among large numbers of people in a peaceful and stable way and of promoting the spirit of self-help, participation, and democratic decision making. Through community development, local action could be linked with macroeconomic development at the national level (Sanders, 1958; Tumin, 1958).

By 1959, AID was assisting twenty-five countries with community development, and was heavily involved, along with the Ford Foundation, in extensive pilot projects in India. The agency had more than 100 advisors assigned to projects and programs throughout the world. From the early 1950s to the early 1960s, AID provided more than $50 million to more than thirty countries through bilateral assistance and indirectly supported community development programs through contributions to United Nations agencies that were funding the movement in nearly thirty other countries (Holdcroft, 1978). Moreover, community development programs were used extensively as ways of preventing or countering insurgency in South Korea, Taiwan, Malaysia, the Philippines, Thailand, and South Vietnam from the late 1950s until the early 1970s.

Despite the widespread acceptance of the community development approach, the programs came under increasing criticism during the late 1950s, often from national planners and macroeconomists, who argued that the primary goal of development was to increase national economic output, and that community development was an economically inefficient means of doing so. By concentrating investment on national production, they argued, "trickle down" and spread effects would increase the incomes of the poor and create surpluses through which government could later provide social services and infrastructure in rural areas. They argued that attention should be focused on lowering population growth rates in developing countries, without which it would be impossible to raise incomes and improve living conditions in communities, no matter how much effort was devoted to local action. Others argued that social change was volatile and unpredictable; once expectations were raised through community development, social dissatisfaction would be difficult to control.

In addition, critics argued that most underdeveloped countries did not have sufficient numbers of "achievement-oriented" leaders or change agents to mobilize and direct community development and, without them, the movement could not succeed (Sanders, 1958).

Both the arguments of the critics and the increasing numbers of disappointing evaluations of the impact of community development led AID in the early 1960s to reduce dramatically its support for such projects. Although it continued to be used as an instrument of counterinsurgency and "pacification" in Vietnam and other countries in Indochina threatened with social unrest until the early 1970s, it was no longer seriously promoted by AID as an instrument of economic development by the mid-1960s.

Indeed, the experience with community development for "pacification" and for building "local democratic institutions" in Vietnam during the late 1960s and early 1970s illustrated many of the problems that had arisen earlier with community development programs in other countries. The Vietnam experience raised long-standing suspicions about the motivations and intentions of the U.S. economic aid program. Community development principles were applied in Vietnam primarily through the Village Self-Development (VSD) program administered jointly by AID and the U.S. military advisory command. Village Self-Development was designed to make small loans and grants to villages in order to generate sufficient local resources to undertake public infrastructure construction and income-generating projects on a self-help basis (Rondinelli, 1971).

The community development program had several major goals. The primary objective was "political development." The loans were intended to bring the benefits of U.S. and Vietnamese government aid to villagers in order to win "the hearts and minds of the people," and allow them to participate in making decisions about the development of their communities. This, according to community development theory, would increase the people's stake in their local and national political systems and strengthen their ability to resist Communist infiltration and insurgency. The loans and grants were made to People's Common Activity Groups (PCAGs), associations of hamlet and village residents created by the community development program. The PCAGs were to be composed of villagers who shared a common perception of their problems and who desired to pursue similar income-generating activities. Only when people learned to work together for common objectives in groups larger than the family unit, U.S. community development and military advisors argued, would they be able to work together in resisting threats and subversion by North Vietnamese guerillas.

Through the PCAGs, villagers were to meet together to choose projects and transmit their selections to village officials for consideration and approval. When all proposals were submitted, priorities would be determined at the annual village general assembly meeting at which all PCAG representatives, as well as other interested residents, would meet with village leaders, to vote on the allocation of VSD funds. Village Self-Development would also increase the responsiveness of local officials—village chiefs, hamlet leaders, and village council chairmen—to the needs of the people and strengthen the peasants' allegiance to the South Vietnamese regime. The program was carried out through the Ministry of Rural Development (MORD) in Saigon.

But Rondinelli (1971), a deputy director of AID's Village Self-Development office from 1970 to 1971, pointed out that the program was ill-fated from the beginning. Progress on community development was slow initially because village, district, and province officials had to be trained, information about the program had to be disseminated to hundreds of villages, groups had to be formed to select and sponsor projects, and hundreds of applications for grants had to be processed. Decentralization of the program required the expansion and improvement of the entire administrative system of local government. Even after projects were chosen, delays in delivering funds were caused by the lack of support for local projects from national and provincial technical services, and by a hierarchy of bureaucrats unconvinced that decentralization and community development were truly the policies of what had been an authoritarian national government.

Continued prodding by MORD and U.S. advisors overcame to some extent the procrastination of technical agencies as the program matured, but technical delays were only outward manifestations of latent political opposition. District and province chiefs in some areas of the country delayed transmitting funds to villages and PCAGs (or diverted them to other uses), ignored information dissemination and training requirements, and procrastinated on approving projects. Even more serious problems resulted from the ingrained distrust of the central government by the rural population. Remnants of the Diem regime's repression of village government authority during the 1950s and the studied disregard for local problems by its military successors reduced the credibility of the central government to its nadir by the late 1960s.

In addition, many of the community development program's requirements were incompatible with Vietnamese customs and traditions. Decisions concerning the future of the village were traditionally the prerogative of the elders and notables and not the responsibility

of all residents or of alien organizations such as PCAGs. Village officials balked at the requirement that they canvass each family to determine its desires and aspirations, claiming that they already knew
their constituents' needs, even if U.S. advisors and officials in Saigon
did not. In some cases, village leaders simply submitted false reports
and chose the projects themselves. Formation of the PCAGs proceeded
slowly in most villages and not at all in others. One village council-
man explained to an AID official that "the villagers here do not understand economic groups and cooperatives. The spirit here is family-
oriented, not group-oriented. Therefore, the VSD program disrupts
the community by bringing on interfamily bickering. The results are
not very good" (Ingle, 1970: 59).

Rondinelli (1971) found that, from the outset, the community development program was plagued by corruption. Diversion of VSD
funds and building materials was widespread, the techniques rang-
ing from favoritism in the approval of projects to outright embezzle-
ment. Experience with VSD highlighted the difference between
Asian and American notions of honesty. Vietnamese ethics, being focused on care of the family, did not define as corrupt many activities
considered to be abusive by Americans. Most Vietnamese did not consider it a crime to divert funds from an unpopular government or a
foreign aid program to better the living conditions of their own
families. This attitude was prevalent especially among civil servants
and military officers who were paid wages insufficient to maintain a
respectable standard of living within their communities. Moreover,
the Oriental tradition of the "squeeze"—the diversion of from 5 to 10
percent of project funds as a charge for facilitating action—was legitimate in the minds of many officials. The only sanction was the "loss of
face" in being caught. With the delegation of VSD management by
many provincial officials to the lower-ranking military officers who
served as district officials in most areas, and the necessity of kicking
back a portion of the diverted funds to province and ministry officials,
the divsersion of funds and materials in 1969 and 1970 was estimated
to have reached 25 to 30 percent of project costs.

In the Montagnard villages in the Central Highlands, Vietnamese district and province officials controlled the selection of projects and the distribution of funds, claiming that the Montagnards
were too primitive and ignorant to manage their own affairs. Few
Montagnard villages ever received the full amount of money that had
been approved for their projects. Abuse was prevalent in animal-
raising projects where district chiefs acted as middlemen, purchasing
animals for the villages at exorbitant prices and taking kickbacks
from the sellers. Contracting for the construction of village projects,

although forbidden by MORD precisely because of the high potential for corruption, was rampant. Inflated costs, faulty construction, favoritism in granting contracts, and kickbacks were all associated with the bidding and contracting procedures.

The experience with AID's community development program in Vietnam also questioned seriously its contribution to political development and counterinsurgency. Rondinelli (1971: 173) found that rather than strengthening villages' resistence to insurgency, community development could succeed only where a substantial amount of security from external threats already existed:

> The most successful community development projects in Vietnam were found in those villages where officials were free from threats of kidnapping and assassination, where village business could be carried on without harassment from insurgent raids and sniper attacks, and where village residents could participate without fear of reprisal and the risks of defending completed projects. An effective system of counterinsurgency seems to be a prerequesite to pacification and development rather than vice versa.

Although AID's community development activities were somewhat more successful in other countries, Holdcroft (1978) points out that the community development movement faded for many of the same reasons that accounted for its demise in Vietnam.

1. Advocates of community development promised to achieve more than the movement could possibly deliver in promoting social stability and improving local living conditions, and thus it generated expectations at both the local and national levels that it could not fulfill.

2. Community development was perceived of by many in the U.S. Congress and by many national leaders as a form of "pacification," aimed at promoting local democratic principles, easing the threats of social instability and subversion, and guiding change in nonrevolutionary ways. Yet, it did not directly address—and indeed, was often designed to divert attention from—the political and social forces that caused and maintained widespread poverty and social dissatisfaction. Often, community development programs strengthened the position of local elites, landowners, and government officials and, as a result, it was difficult to elicit real participation by the disadvantaged.

3. By emphasizing the provision of social services rather than promoting productive and income-generating activities, com-

munity development did not contribute to creating a sound economic base for improving the living conditions of the poor. Resources for both the construction of facilities and for the recurrent costs of social services, therefore, often had to come from central governments that were reluctant or unable to provide them on a large scale throughout the country.

4. Community development programs never solved the problem of coordination, on which their success so heavily depended. The programs required substantial inputs from a variety of government ministries and agencies that did not work together effectively even at the national level. Few community development programs could overcome the ill effects of the rivalries, conflicts, and lack of cooperation among government agencies, and thus activities necessary to the success of community development often could not be coordinated effectively at the local level.

5. Advocates of community development often failed to recognize and to deal with the social heterogeneity in communities and the conflicts among different income, social, and cultural groups in developing countries. They often dealt with communities as groups of people who had common interests and who would work together for the common good. In reality, there was often a multiplicity of differing and conflicting interests, especially between the elites and others, and among people who had always interacted on the basis of family, tribal, ethnic, religious, or other affiliations. Structural barriers were often greater than the incentives offered by community development for cooperation and participation.

6. The "self-help" approach to community development, alone, could not mobilize sufficient resources to promote pervasive and meaningful change and was not an adequate substitute for institutional development.

7. Community development workers were usually recruited from among the more educated and higher income groups, and they tended to support the values and goals of the rural elite more than those of the rural poor. Thus they were not usually effective as leaders or advisors.

8. Often the community development pilot programs were replicated and expanded too rapidly. Community development workers were recruited in large numbers and not given adequate training. When the programs were expanded too widely and too quickly, they could not be supported with the financial and physical resources needed to make them work effectively on a large scale.

Thus, by the late 1960s, the support for community development within AID had largely faded and the movement was displaced by other approaches.

Joint Administration of Development Assistance

Ironically, one of the most successful U.S. foreign aid programs during the 1950s was managed through a process that largely bypassed the usual aid program structure and was administered jointly by the donor and recipient governments through an autonomous agency in the recipient country. The joint administration of development assistance was authorized for U.S. aid to China in 1948 and, with the fall of the mainland to Communist forces in 1949, was transferred to Taiwan. U.S. economic aid for rural and agricultural development to the Republic of China, from 1949 until the late 1960s, was administered by the Sino-American Joint Commission on Rural Reconstruction (JCRR), an autonomous organization consisting of five commissioners, two of whom were appointed by the president of the United States and three by the president of the Republic of China. The JCRR was responsible for administering U.S. loans, grants, and technical assistance for training; crop, forestry, fishery, and livestock production; land and water development, farmers' organizations, agricultural extension, farm credit, farm management, rural health, and related projects (Montgomery, et al., 1964).

The large amount of U.S. aid that went to Taiwan during the 1950s contributed to an annual increase in agricultural productivity of over 6 percent from 1949 to 1961, a 47 percent increase in per capita income during a period of population growth from 1951 and 1960, an increase in fishery production of 250 percent between 1952 and 1960, and a reduction in the crude death rate from 18.2 per 1,000 in 1947 to about 6.7 in 1961. Moreover, with U.S. aid, the JCRR played the central role in strengthening a network of farmers' organizations and providing them with extension services, information, and credit; in carrying out an extensive and successful land reform program that preceeded the "agricultural revolution" in Taiwan; in sending nearly 300 agricultural technicians to the United States for training; and in providing in-service training for more than 55,000 agricultural and health technicians, nearly 12,000 administrators, and more than half a million farmers. The JCRR helped to create a nationwide network of rural health stations in the townships and to support health services in the cities. It also supported a successful family planning program. JCRR commissioners were influential in changing agricultural legislation in Taiwan and in shaping agricultural policy.

Much of the JCRR's success has been attributed to its organization as an autonomous commission, which enabled its leaders to respond quickly to the needs of rural people by providing grants to local "sponsoring agencies." The JCRR staff explored innovative approaches to dealing with development problems, provided technical and administrative assistance to local organizations, and monitored the progress of projects it funded through more than 700 national and local public and private organizations. As Montgomery and his associates (1964: 5) later found, much of the JCRR's effectiveness was due to its joint character, "which enabled it to develop procedures suited to its own operational requirements (and thus to act much more promptly in approving projects, disbursing funds, issuing travel orders, and selecting, hiring, and discharging personnel than either the Chinese government or the AID mission)." Furthermore, as a joint commission, the JCRR was "relatively impervious to political influence and thus able to make decisions on technical and economic grounds and to apply great selectivity in the use of its funds." At the same time, however, its special and prestigious status gave its commissioners and directors direct access to government and private agencies. This political influence helped the JCRR to get resources and cooperation in carrying out its program.

The JCRR's success is also attributed to its strategy of using aid to build the capacity of local organizations to plan and carry out development projects on their own. Unlike the usual process of managing foreign aid in which a central government agency proposes or solicits and then screens and selects projects to be submitted to the AID missions for approval, JCRR obtained project proposals directly from a wide variety of public and private organizations, including community and farmers' organizations. The JCRR staff carefully selected projects that met its overall development objectives and provided technical assistance when it was necessary, but left the implementation entirely to the sponsoring agencies. JCRR audited the funds carefully and made technical inspections, but left project management and control to the sponsors. As a result, Montgomery and his associates (1964: 23) found that:

> Local agencies and organizations of all kinds have benefited from funds and technical advice issuing from the JCRR. In general, however, priority was given in granting technical and financial assistance to development agencies and organizations showing substantial initiative in seeking assistance and possessing the capacity to design and operate appropriate projects. Thus the institutions that already displayed an innovative capability were strengthened. Others lacking only adequate organization were induced to improve their administrative effectiveness, while those lacking initiative

and administrative capability were passed over. . . . By using existing agencies wherever possible in its development activities, JCRR
has strengthened their capacity to implement rural development
projects and to anticipate the needs of their local constituents.

JCRR only financed projects, which were screened by technical
criteria. Among the criteria used for selecting proposals submitted
were that, first, the project satisfied a felt need on the part of rural
people for JCRR's assistance; second, there was a satisfactory arrangement for distributing accrued benefits; third, there was a sponsoring or implementing agency qualified to use JCRR assistance effectively; fourth, the project was financially and technically feasible;
and finally, the project was open to frequent inspections by JCRR
specialists during implementation. The JCRR required all sponsoring agencies to make contributions of cash and voluntary labor to the
projects in accordance with their ability. Project funds had to be segre-
gated in separate accounts and JCRR applied simple but stringent financial procedures and auditing controls to assure their proper allocation and use.

Joint administration of development assistance in Taiwan had
many advantages. It gave the JCRR the independence and flexibility
to take action quickly and to plan programs that were uniquely tailored to local and national needs. The cooperative arrangement allowed Chinese and U.S. officials to compromise on conflicting political
interests and to make joint decisions with a minimum of ill feeling.
JCRR's independence also allowed it to make decisions by technical
criteria and to avoid the "pork barrel" approach of selecting projects
and distributing funds on the basis of political pressure. Moreover, its
flexibility and independence allowed the JCRR to work directly with
"grass roots" organizations, thereby strengthening their capacity to
promote development at the local level. Its autonomy led to a high degree of continuity in JCRR's policies and programs but also to continuing experimentation and innovation. As an organization outside of
the regular government structure, JCRR was able to offer higher
salaries and benefits to attract the most talented and skilled personnel.

Although the JCRR proved to be an extremely effective arrangement for administering U.S. foreign aid and for promoting widespread
development in Taiwan, Montgomery and his associates (1964: 5)
found that "these immediate and long-term accomplishments were
not achieved without some sacrifice." As they pointed out, there were
resentments from the AID Mission at JCRR's free-wheeling capacity
to respond to requests for assistance outside the usual program and
technical channels and, at times, from agencies of the Chinese Government at JCRR's apparently preferred position and public prestige.
The enthusiasm for and the degree of support enjoyed by JCRR fluc-

tuated with the ebb and flow of American personnel assigned to the AID Mission and with new policy directives from Washington. At times JCRR felt its very life threatened by American indifferences, for example, during an 18-month period when both American Commissioner positions were left vacant.

Pointing out that joint administration of U.S. foreign aid was successful in Taiwan, Montgomery and his associates nevertheless cautioned that this arrangement required many preconditions that had existed or were developed in this particular country and that its effective use in other developing countries depended on creating similar conditions. These conditions include strong political commitment and support for development activities and for an autonomous agency to fund them, the ability to staff the autonomous agency with highly competent technical and managerial staff, a willingness on the part of national leaders to delegate substantial authority to the joint organization, and the capacity to mobilize local support for its activities. Moreover, the "sponsoring agency" approach used by JCRR was crucial to its success in building local institutions and distributing the benefits of aid funds widely in rural areas. A network of local organizations had to be created or strengthened to participate in the development process. Finally, the joint arrangement seemed to work best when both the donor and recipient countries appointed highly competent, honest, and experienced leaders to the organization.

Perhaps JCRR's success was only really apparent in retrospect, but little attempt was made by ICA and its successors to replicate this joint arrangement for administering development assistance. "It is a strange fact that JCRR seems to have engendered no important resentments except among some AID personnel," Montgomery and his colleagues (1964: 71) concluded. "Perhaps future joint operations will require change more in American practice than in that of the cooperating country." They noted that experiments in joint operations "will not provide a solution for all the technical and political problems that plague American foreign aid. But they may yield important results in selective areas, and their successes may point the way to more general improvements in U.S. performance elsewhere."

The Political Development and Institution-building Approaches

By the early 1960s, U.S. foreign assistance began to expand, due in part to the election of President John F. Kennedy and to his administration's strong interest in international affairs. Seeing the potential for foreign aid to achieve basic social and economic goals that were compatible with foreign policy interests, Kennedy asked Congress in 1961 to replace the Mutual Security Act of 1951 with a foreign aid program that would separate military from economic aid and to increase technical and capital assistance to the poor countries of the world. Kennedy told Congress that "there exists in the 1960s an historic opportunity for a major economic assistance effort by the free industrialized nations to move more than half the people of the less developed nations into self-sustained economic growth" (CQS, 1965: 186).

The Foreign Assistance Act of 1961 provided funds for development loans, development grants, and investment surveys. It abolished the International Cooperation Agency and the Development Loan Fund and transferred their functions to a new semi autonomous organization under the supervision of the State Department—the Agency for International Development (AID).

Congress declared in the Foreign Assistance Act of 1961 that "it is not only expressive of our sense of freedom, justice, and compassion but also important to our national security that the United States, through private as well as public efforts, assist the people of less developed countries in their efforts to acquire the knowledge and resources essential for development and to build the economic, political and social institutions which will meet their aspirations for a better life, with freedom, and in peace."

To achieve these objectives, Congress outlined specific guidelines for foreign assistance, many of which restated the principles inherent in U.S. foreign aid since the time of the Marshall Plan. Congress declared that:

First, development is primarily the responsibility of the people of less developed countries themselves. Assistance from the United States shall be used in support of, rather than in subistitution for, the self-help efforts that are essential to successful development programs, and shall be concentrated in those countries that take positive steps to help themselves.

Second, the tasks of successful development in some instances require the active involvement and cooperation of many countries on a multilateral basis.

Third, assistance shall be utilized to encourage regional cooperation by less developed countries in the solution of common problems and the development of shared resources.

Fourth, the first objectives of assistance shall be to support the efforts of less developed countries to meet the fundamental needs of their peoples for sufficient food, good health, home ownership and decent housing, and the opportunity to gain the basic knowledge and skills required to make their own way forward to a brighter future. In supporting these objectives, particular emphasis shall be placed on utilization of resources for food production and voluntary family planning.

Fifth, assistance shall wherever practicable be constituted of United States commodities and services furnished in a manner consistent with other efforts of the United States to improve its balance of payments position.

Sixth, assistance shall be furnished in such a manner as to promote efficiency and economy in operation so that the United States obtains maximum possible effectiveness for each dollar spent.

In addition to loans and grants for industrial development, agriculture, population, health, education, transportation, public administration, and other sectors, the Foreign Assistance Act of 1961 also provided funds for housing guarantees to facilitate and increase the participation of private enterprise in housing construction and for U.S. schools, libraries, and hospitals abroad. Special provisions were made for assisting family planning and population growth control programs in developing countries.

After taking office, Kennedy also began to pursue a new relationship with Latin American countries, and in 1961 the United States participated in the creation of the Alliance for Progress, the first coordinated multinational effort to bring about social, economic and political development in Latin America. The charter signed by twenty member governments of the Organization of American States called for each country in Latin America to prepare a national plan within eighteen months with consistent targets for expanding productive capacity in industry, agriculture, mining, transport, power, and communications, and for improving urban and rural living conditions through investments in housing, education, and health over the next decade. The Alliance sought to generate $100 billion of investment in Latin America. Although there was some debate within the Kennedy administration over how United States aid for the Alliance was to be provided, Kennedy's advisors saw the opportunity to use the strong political support in Congress for Latin American development to bolster the entire foreign aid budget. They assigned the administration of the Alliance program to the Latin America Bureau of AID. In addition to receiving a larger budget, AID was authorized to hire a large new staff to administer the program in Washington. It expanded its missions in eighteen South American countries and created a new subregional office in Central America and a special office to coordinate its assistance for the development of the Brazilian northeast (Levinson and deOnis, 1970).

Political Modernization and Development Administration

New approaches to development administration emerged during the 1960s, partly in reaction to the inadequacies of the technology transfer and community development processes, and partly in response to challenges emerging from new concepts and theories. The Ford Foundation sponsored, through the Comparative Administration Group (CAG) of the American Society for Public Administration, a series of theoretical studies on administrative and political reform in developing nations. The CAG consisted, as one of its founders (Riggs, 1971: 5) pointed out, "largely of scholars who had served on technical cooperation missions in many parts of the third world, under conditions which showed the accepted administrative doctrines of American practice to be severely limited in their applicability to different cultural situations."

The CAG participants believed that fundamental political and administrative changes were needed in developing countries to prepare them to deal with the political and social changes implied by development. The political modernizers believed that the transfer of U.S. administrative procedures and techniques was not sufficient. Simply improving the efficiency of existing bureaucracies in developing countries was inadequate to create the preconditions for rapid economic growth and social modernization (Gable, 1975). The scholars who participated in CAG focused their attention on three sets of issues: the political dimensions of development administration, the process of development planning, and the performance of administrative systems in developing countries (Esman, 1971). Summarizing the thinking of many political and social scientists who were involved in development studies during the 1960s, Huntington (1971) described nine major characteristics of political modernization. It was a revolutionary process involving a radical and total change in patterns of human life, a complex process involving changes in virtually all areas of human behavior, a systematic process in which changes in one area are related to and affected changes in other areas of society, and a lengthy process that could only be worked out over time. Also, political modernization was seen as a global process in the sense that all societies were either modern or in the process of becoming so. The process was phased—all societies moved through the same basic stages. The process was thought to be homogenizing in that it pushed societies toward the same basic political and social tendencies. It was also thought to be irreversible: although rates of change varied and there were temporary breakdowns, the direction of change was inevitably toward modernization. Finally, political modernization was considered to be a progressive process—not only inevitable, but also desirable. Thus the task of development administration was to facilitate and accelerate the process of political modernization.

Those scholars who participated in CAG saw development administration as a set of activities fundamentally different from routine public administration. They viewed development administration as "social engineering" and national governments—rather than local communities—as the prime movers of social change. A good deal of effort, therefore, went into defining development administration and into attempting to create a theoretical framework for studies of comparative politics and administration so that general principles and models could be developed.

The problem of definition proved to be more difficult than expected and, although some consensus emerged about the nature of development administration activities, no single definition was adopted by the group. Underlying all of the definitions was the concept that development administration was concerned with promoting change. Landau (1970) defined development administration as a "directive and directional process which is intended to make things happen in a certain way over intervals of time." Others perceived it as a means of improving the capacities of central governments to deal with problems and opportunities created by modernization and change (Lee, 1970; Spengler, 1963). For Gant (1966: 200) development administration was "that aspect of public administration in which the focus of attention is on organizing and administering public agencies in such a way as to stimulate and facilitate defined programs of social and economic progress." Its central feature, Esman (1972: 1) contended, was "the role of governmental administration in inducing, guiding and managing the interrelated processes of nation building, economic growth and societal change."

National development administration would be the instrument of transforming traditional societies. Weidner (1964: 200) argued that development administration "is a process of guiding an organization toward the achievement of development objectives. It is action-oriented, and it places administration at the center in facilitating the attainment of development objectives." But, unless the entire political system was reformed and modernized, governments of developing nations could not adequately direct and control social and economic progress. Thompson (1964) insisted that the objectives of development administration were to create in developing countries an innovative and cosmopolitan atmosphere in which widely shared planned goals could be made operational and in which action and planning could be combined. He saw the goal of development administration as creating a society in which influence could be diffused, toleration for interdependence could be created, and bureaupathology could be avoided. "What is urgently needed in the study of development administration," Riggs (1970: 108) argued, "is a new set of doctrines likely to prove helpful to countries who seek to enhance these capacities in order to be able to undertake with success programs intended to modify the characteristics of their physical, human, and cultural environments."

Although the CAG's work remained somewhat abstract and had little real influence on AID projects and programs, it did create an awareness of the importance of political development and administrative modernization.

The Institution-building Approach

Perhaps of more direct significance to the AID program, was a new approach to development administration that emerged during the 1960s and early 1970s, in part from the work of the Comparative Administration Group on theories of political modernization and administrative reform. This approach was called "institution building." The concepts of and approaches to institution building were formulated by Milton Esman and colleagues at schools participating in the Midwest Universities Consortium for International Activities (MUCIA). The institution-building approach was heavily funded by AID and tested through AID-sponsored field projects.

The institution-building approach emerged at a time when many of the conventional growth-maximization and industrialization theories of development were coming under severe criticism. By the early 1960s, it had become increasingly clear that foreign aid programs promoting rapid growth through capital intensive industrialization simply were not working in most developing countries. Growth occurred in some Third World nations during the 1950s and early 1960s, but at rates well below those targeted in national development plans. Studies found that foreign aid had little direct impact on increasing the levels of GNP in most developing countries and, in some, had simply reinforced polarizing tendencies in which a small minority of the elites got richer while the vast majority of the people remained poor (Friedman, 1958; Griffin and Enos, 1970).

The problems, it was argued, arose from the vast numbers of obstacles and bottlenecks to industrial and agricultural expansion in developing countries. The primary task of governments and international assistance agencies, therefore, was to overcome these obstacles and to break the bottlenecks so that economic, social, and political changes could create conditions more conducive to development.

Foreign assistance would have to be focused on the key sectors in which the bottlenecks occurred and on key problems that created obstacles to increased public and private investment. U.S. foreign assistance programs concentrated on providing technical and financial assistance for research into new high-yield seed varieties, irrigation system construction, improvements in agricultural training and extension programs, the creation of marketing systems, the organization of cooperatives and farmers associations, and the initiation of agricultural credit schemes. Land reform and ownership redistribution programs were strongly advocated. Large amounts of U.S. foreign aid went to private and voluntary organizations promoting population control and family planning in developing nations. Aid was also channelled into human resources development, primarily through programs to assist developing countries to strengthen their educational institutions.

The low level of administrative capacity in governments of developing countries was seen as a serious obstacle or bottleneck to development. One of the leading U.S. development administration theorists, Donald Stone (1965: 53) argued, that "the primary obstacles to development are administrative rather than economic, and not deficiencies in natural resources." He summarized the arguments of many other development theorists in noting that poor countries "generally lack the administrative capability for implementing plans and programs," and that in the United States and other economically advanced countries "a great deal of untapped knowledge and experience is available in respect to the development of effective organizations to plan and administer comprehensive development programs." But, he insisted, "most persons charged with planning and other development responsibilities in individual countries, as well as persons made available under technical assistance programs, do not have adequate knowledge or adaptability in designing and installing organizations, institutions, and procedures suitable for a particular country."

The institution-building approach was based on the assumption that the introduction of change was the primary purpose of development administration. Indeed, development was defined as "a process involving the introduction of change or innovations in societies" (Smart, 1970). In developing countries, the most urgent need of governments was for administrative procedures and methods that promoted change and not for those that simply strengthened its maintenance functions. Underlying this approach was the assumption that change was introduced and sustained primarily through formal institutions and especially through government and educational organizations (Esman, 1967; Blase, 1973). In order for changes to be adopted and have a long term impact, they had to be protected by formal organizations—that is, change had to be "institutionalized." The process of institutionalizing change involved a complex set of interactions between the organization adopting or promoting change and the environment in which it had to operate and obtain support.

According to Esman (1967) the variables that affected the ability of organizations to institutionalize change included: (1) leadership—a group of persons who engage actively in formulating an organization's doctrine and programs and who direct its operations and interactions with the environment; (2) doctrine—the organization's values, objectives, and operational methods that rationalize its actions; (3) program—the functions and services that constitute the organization's output; (4) resources—the organization's physical, human, and technological inputs; and (5) structure—the processes established for the operation and maintenance of the organization.

Each of these aspects of an institution had to be strengthened if it was to be effective in introducing, protecting, and sustaining change. Also, an effective change-inducing institution had to engage successfully in transactions with other organizations in its environment in order to obtain authority, resources, and support, and to make the impact of change felt throughout society. Those transactions occurred through an institution's linkages. Four types of linkages had to be strengthened: (1) enabling linkages with organizations controlling resources and authority needed by the institution to function effectively; (2) functional linkages with organizations performing complementary functions and services or which are competitive with the institution; (3) normative linkages through which other organizations place constraints on or legitimate the institutions' norms and values as expressed in its doctrine or programs; and, (4) diffused linkages through which the institution has an impact on other organizations in the environment.

The transactions allow the institution to gain support and overcome resistance, exchange resources, structure the environment, and transfer norms and values (Esman, 1967). An organization became an institution when the changes that it advocated and protected were accepted, valued, and became functional in the environment. Then institution building was accomplished (Smart, 1970).

The AID-sponsored activities included a massive research program into ways of building institutional capability for development. They also included technical assistance to institutions in several developing countries. The research produced detailed and extensive studies of organizational characteristics and administrative behavior in developing nations (Eaton, 1972).

The results of the technical assistance, however, were somewhat disappointing. Drawing on four specific cases (Siffin, 1967; Birkhead, 1967; Hanson, 1968; and Blase and Rodriguez, 1968) that were typical of many others in which the universities attempted to apply institution building theory, Blase (1973: 8-9) notes that nearly all the technical aid came from the faculty of U.S. universities who were only able to introduce models of change and were "unable to carry their local counterparts with them on significant issues." Studies of the cases in Nigeria, Ecuador, Thailand, and Turkey indicated that the local counterparts tended to support only a few of the institutional changes that were recommended by foreign assistance personnel. "Local staff members frequently attached higher priority to protecting existing relationships than to the changes proposed by technical assistance personnel," Blase concluded, "although they frequently agreed with technical personnel about proposed goals."

Reassessment of Public Administration Experience

Ironically, during the 1970s, the administrative-political reform and the institution-building approaches came under heavy attack both by administrative theorists, who considered them unsystematic and insufficiently theoretical to add much to knowledge about comparative administration (Loveman, 1976; Sigelman, 1976; Bendor, 1976), and by practitioners, who considered them too abstract and theoretical to be operational (Ingle, 1979). Although they generated a great deal of intellectual stimulation among the participants in the CAG and institution-building projects, the research never led to an academically acceptable theoretical framework for studies of comparative politics and comparative administration. Warren Ilchman (1971: 44), a participant in CAG, concluded that the group never lived up to "the promise of discovering through comparative analysis methods and approaches what would be useful in development situations."

To some degree, AID officials' thinking about the field of development administration was influenced by the Ford Foundation's reassessment of its attempts to strengthen public administration in developing countries during the 1960s. In the early 1970s, the Ford Foundation did a general evaluation of the institutes of public administration that it had helped to establish and an in-depth assessment of its program in Nigeria, where it had provided more than $8 million in financial assistance for a program aimed at assisting the Nigerians to cope with the problems of "an expatriate infused bureaucracy, requiring 'localization'; a colonial-inherited bureaucratic structure which was not change-oriented; inadequate output of university graduates with administrative and management skills; a complex and now Federated governing system presenting unresolved problems of coordination, resources allocation vis-à-vis the separate States, budgeting and local government; and, inadequate capacity for social science research" (Edwards, 1972: 2).

As AID had done in other countries, the Ford Foundation financed in-service training programs in Nigeria through Staff Development Centers, provided preservice training through the Ife Institute of Administration and offered technical assistance in designing the National Plan for 1962-1968. It supported public administration professional organizations and conferences, built up the capacity for social and economic research in training institutes, provided assistance with administration and management for many development projects, and helped create the Nigerian Institute of Management.

However, the evaluations concluded that conditions within the Nigerian government had further deteriorated during the 1960s despite massive aid for improving public administration. The recommendations for administrative reform went largely unheeded. Among the preliminary findings were that "rapid 'locatization' tended to stabilize the bureaucracy, fixing concerns for internal status and influence, which did not encourage change." Policy making continued to be dominated by a change-resistant bureaucracy, notwithstanding the rise of the military to political power. Macroeconomic planning became even less relevant than before because the planners and economists had not linked plans to programs, budgets, projects, and sound management practices. Problems of poor coordination and centralization had grown with federalism. Parastatal organizations, especially marketing boards, had increased in number and had become more difficult to manage. New opportunities for education and training produced an elitist attitude among university graduates and enterprise leaders. The report (Edwards, 1972) pointed out that "growing financial resources—chiefly oil revenues—have eased financial and resource constraints but conversely have multiplied demands upon scarce and inadequately trained manpower for administration and management, at all levels of government."

Other evaluations later found that the training institutions, created at high cost, were able to provide services only to a small percentage of the civil servants needing training and that few were able to carry out research effectively or to provide consulting services to the government. By the end of the 1960s, little evidence existed to document their impact on improving administrative capacities or performance in the governments of countries in which they were established (Paul, 1983).

AID officials' discussions with Ford Foundation evaluators during the early 1970s led them to examine U.S. bilateral assistance for public administration training and institution building. They came to similar conclusions. "Fairly conventional public administration methods had been used, as conceived by U.S. university contractors," they observed. These methods offered "too academic an approach in the context of conventional U.S.-oriented public administration." The universities had "spotty recruitment records in terms of continuity and quality, relying chiefly on U.S. academics." They usually created a "separate U.S. contract 'team' presence, with excessive reliance upon expatriate heads of assisted institutions." Inadequate attention was given to expanding the pool of trained manpower and their approach to institution building did not effectively strengthen the linkages of the assisted organizations to leadership, support, and the political environment. Finally, the report concluded, the insitutions that were assisted never developed a strong research capacity (Edwards, 1972).

Both the AID and the Ford Foundation evaluators agreed that more innovative programs and approaches to technical assistance were needed in developing countries, that the assistance had to be focused more directly on operational problems, and that training had to be tailored more closely to the internal problems and needs of the developing countries rather than simply providing those programs in which U.S. universities had developed expertise.

AID reassessed its support of public administration assistance at the end of the 1960s and decided at the beginning of the 1970s to cut back both its funding for public administration training and for research and technical assistance in administrative reform and institution building.

3

Sectoral and Project
Systems Management

The U.S. foreign aid program was in serious political difficulty by the mid-1960s. An increasing amount of economic and military aid was being channeled to South Vietnam at a time when the war was becoming unpopular and when many congressmen and senators feared that they were losing influence over foreign affairs to the White House. Charges of waste, inefficiency, and poor management were leveled against many AID projects in Asia and Latin America. The backlash against the Vietnam war led Congress, in 1967, to cut AID's budget to the lowest level since the United States began giving economic aid to foreign governments in 1947. In an attempt to exercise stronger supervision over the aid program, Congress refused to give advance authorization for spending in fiscal year 1969, and withdrew authorizations previously enacted for development loan funds for the Alliance for Progress. Congress placed increasing numbers of restrictions on foreign aid spending, and required the termination of aid to countries that increased their defense spending to levels that "materially interfered with economic growth."

The cutbacks in foreign aid budgets during the late 1960s and early 1970s were a reaction not only to the Vietnamese war, but also to increasing criticism of the Alliance for Progress. Although by 1967, more than $115 billion had been invested in Latin America, more than 88 percent of which came from the Latin American countries themselves, and less than 7 percent had come from the United States, progress in meeting the Alliance's economic and social objectives had been disappointingly slow. Between 1961 and 1968, the U.S. aid program had committed a total of nearly $10 billion in economic assistance to the region. More than half of that assistance had been channeled through AID in the form of repayable program loans to help Brazil, Chile, and Colombia to import goods from the United States; sector loans to other countries for dealing with problems of agriculture, education, and health; and project loans that funded specific activities such as road building, agricultural research, industrial development, and energy production (CQS, 1969).

But managing aid to the Alliance for Progress turned out to be more complicated and difficult than AID Latin America Bureau staff had anticipated. In reality, few Latin American countries had projects adequately prepared for borrowing, and feasibility analyses were often done hastily in order to get AID loan funds committed. Usually, project proposals were hurried to make the end of the fiscal year obligation deadline, resulting in a "June bulge" in the number of projects submitted. Levinson and deOnis (1970: 115), who had done an extensive study of the Alliance, observed that each year,

> by the end of June, the AID loan staff would produce a pile of loan proposals for authorization. This task was more desperate and difficult than it seemed. The perennially understaffed missions in the various countries were dealing for the most part with underdeveloped borrowers and Latin American law. For example, AID routinely required of borrowers a statement that they had the legal authority to enter into a loan and carry out its terms and conditions. But it often took months to get this statement from a ministry of finance that did not have a full-time legal staff. The AID standard loan agreement had other clauses totally unfamiliar to lawyers in a different legal system. Solving all of these problems took time. And because new programs did not get started until late in the fiscal year, authorizations were late again the next year.

The rush to submit authorizations for loans at the end of each fiscal year made AID's congressional oversight committees suspicious that the agency was funding badly planned and financially unsound projects and programs. "And in some cases these charges were well founded," Levinson and deOnis (1970: 115) discovered. "Congressional cutbacks in funds and refusal to agree to a long-term commitment made the AID administrators feel that Congress was not really committed to the Alliance. AID's late authorizations, on the other hand, made Congress even more reluctant to authorize more funds. Mistrust escalated on both sides."

Although progress was made in meeting the educational and health goals set out by the Alliance in 1961, economic and political improvements were more difficult to discern. The average increase in per capita gross domestic product among Alliance countries between 1961 and 1967 was about 1.3 percent, well below the target rate of 2.5

percent. Increases in industrial output were negligible, and agricultural output barely kept pace with population growth. Most land reform programs met strong political opposition and little change resulted from efforts to redistribute income. Housing construction was less than 10 percent of the level targeted by the Alliance. Moreover, few countries adopted more democratic political systems; indeed, military regimes strengthened their hold in Latin America during the 1960s. Criticism of the Alliance became an issue in the 1968 presidential election in which the Republican candidate, Richard M. Nixon, called for a "sweeping re-evaluation of its activities" (CQS, 1969).

Congressional distrust of the foreign aid program deepened when the Administrator of AID, William Gaud, who had been appointed in 1964, attempted to protect the rising levels of spending in Vietnam by recommending to the Budget Bureau that cuts in the foreign assistance program be taken from the spending authorizations for the Alliance for Progress. The Budget Bureau refused. Gaud told USAID mission directors in Latin America that he thought the Alliance had been overfunded by Congress. When congressional foreign aid committees learned of the speech, it raised their determination to cut Alliance funds (Levinson and deOnis, 1970). In 1968, Congress cut the foreign aid budget to a new low, reducing by half the Johnson administration's $750 million request for development loans, and made deep cuts in the Alliance for Progress budget.

Further, during the late 1960s, both multilateral and bilateral foreign assistance programs came under increasing criticism by several international commissions. The Pearson commission (1969) and the Jackson committee (1969) took the assistance policies of AID, the World Bank, and the United Nations to task for their complexity and rigidity, and for not recognizing the great differences in needs among developing countries. Among the Jackson committee's most severe criticisms was that foreign aid was not tailored to local conditions. Most international and bilateral assistance programs merely transferred Western practices and institutions to poor countries without modifying or adapting them. "Instead of measuring and cutting the cloth on the spot in accordance with individual circumstances and wants," the committee claimed, "a ready-made garment is produced and forced to fit afterwards" (Jackson, 1969: 171). Moreover, foreign assistance programs were focused almost entirely on promoting rapid macroeconomic growth and had not taken into consideration the distributional effects of economic development policies. Thus they had largely ignored the masses of people living in poverty whose conditions were worsening rather than improving.

At the same time, a recurring complaint by officials in AID and other international assistance organizations was that developing countries still lacked the administrative capacity to plan and implement projects and programs in those sectors that presented the strongest obstacles to development. In an influential book on national development planning, World Bank official Albert Waterston (1965) had argued that "there is generally a scarcity of well-prepared projects ready to go and it is hard to find coherent programs for basic economic and social sectors. The lack of projects reduces the number of productive investment opportunities."

The Control-oriented Management Approach Within AID

In reaction to the widespread criticism of bilateral and multilateral foreign aid programs that were reflected in the findings of the Pearson and Jackson reports, and because of increased scrutiny and oversight of the AID program by Congress, the agency began in the late 1960s and early 1970s to adopt new management systems for its own lending and grant activities. The system of controls and management procedures adopted by AID was influenced in part by the need to integrate project development activities and documentation with the agency's budgeting process and with its annual congressional presentation. Adoption of a more systematic approach to loan and grant management was also influenced by the prevailing belief at the end of the 1960s in the efficacy of "systems management." Many administrative theorists argued that implementation could be greatly improved by the application of project management systems that had been used in private corporations to manage large-scale construction projects and in the Defense Department and NASA to manage defense systems and space projects. Indeed, a number of other federal agencies had also adopted planning-budgeting-programming systems (PPBS), of which AID's planning-budgeting-and-review (PBAR) process was but a variation.

The management science approach, strongly advocated by technical experts, project engineers, and management consultants was one, as Esman and Montgomery (1969) pointed out, "which applies mathematical logic to optimizing the performance of an organization, usually in cost-effectiveness terms. . . . These methods include the following elements: detailed identification of the interrelated factors in a complex system of action; precise time phasing of related activities, and control of operations through the use of modern high-speed communication and reporting instruments." Cost-benefit analyses, quantitative analyses for decision making, CPM-PERT scheduling and control techniques, and management information systems were also prescribed. AID's PBAR process described a detailed system of procedures for its entire project cycle, concentrating on the stages from project identification to approval and on logistics of implementation—especially budgeting, contracting and procurement—and evaluation. The PBAR process, depicted in Figure 3.1, was expected to integrate and unify the systems used for grant and loan projects, resulting in improved project design and development; integrate AID's project planning and budgeting procedures, thereby reducing the growing divergence between the agency's congressional presentations and the programs for which it requested appropriations; and allow the agency to make more systematic and coordinated decisions about the selection of projects.

USAID missions would be required to submit a brief Project Identification Document (PID) for each project proposal. The PID would describe how the project related to the mission's overall development program for the country and the country's national and sectoral development plans. The PID would identify the primary beneficiaries of the project; provide preliminary information on the activities of other donors in the sector for which the project was being proposed, and describe more detailed analyses and studies that would have to be done to develop the proposal. The PID would also have to include a rough estimate of total cost and the time period for implementation, along with estimates of the amount of inputs that could be expected from the host country government and other donors.

The PIDs would be reviewed by relevant technical and regional bureaus within the agency and by AID's budget office. Those PIDs that were approved, could be developed by the USAID missions into Project Review Papers (PRPs). The project review papers would expand on and develop the information provided in the PIDs and provide sufficiently detailed financial information and time schedules so that AID officials could decide whether or not to include the proposed project in the requested appropriations for the next fiscal year.

Those projects for which PRPs were approved could be further developed into full-scale proposals, or Project Papers (PPs). The project papers would provide a definitive description, design and appraisal of the project and describe plans for project implementation and evaluation.

The project papers would have to provide detailed information on the amounts of loans or grants needed from AID, total program or project costs, and resources that would be provided by the sponsoring or implementing agencies in the developing country. The PPs would

Figure 3.1   Interaction of Major Agency Processes

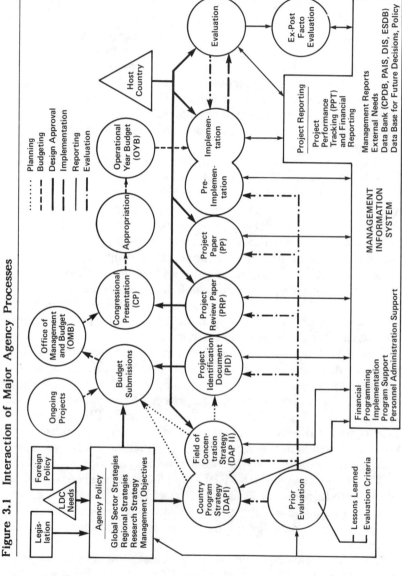

also include a detailed justification for the project and the preparation of a "log-frame" design.

The "log-frame," or logical framework, was a device designed for AID by a management consulting firm, Practical Concepts Incorporated (PCI), to formulate projects in a consistent, comprehensive, and "rational" way. It required USAID missions to describe the projects by their goals, purposes, outputs, and inputs, providing for each "objectively verifiable indicators" by which progress could be measured and evaluated. In addition, the project designers would have to describe the important assumptions they were making about each aspect of the project that might affect implementation. All of this information would be summarized in a matrix format that would allow reviewers and evaluators to assess the "logical framework" of each project. The log-frame would require USAID missions to design each project comprehensively and in detail prior to final approval of funds.

In addition, the project papers had to contain an analysis of the project's background—the history and development of the proposal, a description of how the proposed project related to other projects being implemented by the mission and host country government, an analysis of policies and programs in the sector, and a summary of the findings of studies done of the problem that the project would attempt to solve. The part of the project paper that was considered most important to agency officials was the project analysis, which would include an economic analysis of the effects of the project on intended beneficiaries, on other groups, and on the national economy; technical feasibilty analysis of the project design; "social soundness" analysis of the project's impact on the sociocultural traditions and values of the groups that would be affected by it; and analysis of host country government policies (tax system, credit rates, pricing, and regulatory structures) that might affect the success of the project. In addition, the analyses would include an assessment of the government's financial capacity to implement the project successfully, and cost-benefit or internal rate of return analyses of project tasks. The project paper was to include an assessment of the administrative ability of the implementing institutions to carry out the tasks described in the prospectus.

Moreover, the project paper had to include a detailed implementation plan providing a programming schedule for all tasks and activities, "milestone" indicators of progress, a schedule for disbursement of AID funds and procurement of needed inputs, and a plan for monitoring, reporting, and evaluation.

In those areas where the USAID mission thought there were weaknesses in the host country government's capacity to carry out the project, or where policies might adversely affect the successful completion of it, the staff could recommend conditions and covenants pre-scribing changes that the government would have to make before re-ceiving an AID loan or grant.

Guidelines, procedures, required forms, and controls for each stage of the PBAR cycle were included in a detailed set of Manual Or-ders and in AID's *Project Assistance Handbook*.

The "Key Problems" Focus of Management Assistance

Also in response to criticisms of foreign assistance and in reaction to the growing dissatisfaction among AID's own administrative experts, the agency's Office of Development Administration undertook a broad survey of AID's experience during the 1950s and 1960s to identify the "key problems of development administration" that it should address during the 1970s. The report noted that "two decades of assistance to developing nations have provided significant improvements in their administrative systems. Yet deficiencies in managerial capacity are greater than ever. It has become increasingly apparent that national development programs, whether in family planning, education, or business, too often fall short of expectations, for reasons of manage-rial weakness" (Koteen et al., 1970: 1).

The report suggested that AID redirect its development adminis-tration activities to provide a strategic orientation that would focus on pragmatic problems of administration. Assistance would be aimed at decision makers in key development programs—and not just at ad-ministrative specialists—in order to increase their capacity for man-aging change and development rather than simply for achieving econ-omy and efficiency. It would also attempt to promote more effectively the distribution of appropriate technology for public purposes; de-velop institutions that were "closer to the people," that is, those that facilitate devolution of decision making and control of administration from the center; and, harness and disseminate appropriate manage-ment and related behavioral technologies. In addition, AID would seek to strengthen the government's ability to cooperate more closely with private organizations.

The report noted a number of serious administrative problems in developing countries that AID would have to address. One of the most serious was the shortage of qualified managerial personnel to cope with the demands of change and modernization. AID's survey led its staff to conclude that the content of overseas public administration and management training programs were inappropriate and obso-lete. In addition, there were "few programs for senior executives, lack of managerial (as opposed to professional and technical) training, and lack of continuous staff training in management that blends formal and informal education." These problems were aggravated by the shortage of adequate numbers of trained teachers and trainers, and the lack of appropriate research and teaching materials. In addition, most developing countries lacked institutional capacity for management education and training, especially in the form of professional schools and "intermediate training institutions."

Another serious problem identified by AID's survey was the need for improvement in "the relevance, effectiveness, and performance of key development institutions" (Koteen et al., 1970: 24). These were manifested in the reluctance of government institutions in developing countries to promote and sustain change, their slow adaptation to change, the lack of cooperation among them, and inadequate awareness and application of institution-building methods.

Moreover, a crucial problem for AID was the inability of governments in developing countries to plan and manage projects effectively. This weakness was due to lack of high-level administrative and political support for many projects, the failure to enact appropriate supporting policies, and the inability to use modern management techniques to design and implement development programs.

The staff of AID's Office of Development Administration saw an urgent need for creating an institutionalized project management process in developing countries that linked planning, budgeting, and financial activities, and that promoted cooperation among the technical offices that were responsible for project implementation. They saw a need to go beyond the economic and financial techniques that had been used most frequently to design and appraise income-producing projects during the Point Four era, and to include in the project-planning framework new organizational and managerial techniques, manpower planning methods, behavioral analyses, and problem-solving procedures that were more appropriate in the social development projects that AID was now funding. Furthermore, AID and other international agencies had, in the past, concentrated almost entirely on assisting developing countries with project preparation and appraisal, but a growing need in many developing countries was for assistance with project implementation.

Finally, a most serious development problem was the inadequacy of local government and the field services of central ministries to deliver services and new technology to the people. In most developing countries, AID's survey found, the strengthening of local government had low priority and national institutions had little capacity to assist local governments. Local administrative units lacked both the financial resources to provide services and the managerial capacity to maintain and expand existing ones. The survey found little evidence of cooperation between local and national governments in promoting development, of effective planning or managerial capacity at the regional level, or of popular participation in development activities.

The "Key Problems in Development Administration" report provided the guiding principles for AID's development management assistance during the first half of the 1970s. Priorities included: (1) improving sector-oriented management capability in developing countries through technical aid and training; (2) improving the concepts and methods of project management within a systematic framework by developing appropriate training materials and programs; (3) assessing and improving the capacity of local and national governments to deliver services to people in developing countries; and (4) finding ways of promoting popular participation in project and program implementation, especially for those groups that AID came to define as the primary targets for its assistance.

The Sectoral Systems Managment Approach

Thus, in the early 1970s, AID began to concentrate its resources on improving management in "key development sectors." The agency had begun to focus U.S. foreign assistance on four high-priority fields: agriculture and food production, nutrition and health, population and family planning, and education and human resource development. The new sector orientation, as officials of the Office of Development Administration pointed out, "represents a major shift away from attempts to improve public bureaucracy in general with better staff services, organization and administrative technique. It features a sharper, more limited and actionable focus on the management requirements of substantive programs to solve specific development problems" (USAID, 1973: 3).

The new approach would be concerned with broader administrative problems only to the extent that they presented direct obstacles to improving sectoral management. AID's technical and financial assistance would focus on: (1) using simplified systems approaches and behavioral analyses for improving the design, creation or control of systems of action; (2) lowering the cost of delivering appropriate technology and supporting services in the agricultural and health sectors; (3) helping "clientele groups" to mobilize their own resources and use external resources to obtain needed services; (4) promoting collaboration between public and private institutions in achieving sectoral development goals; and (5) improving the management of AID's own sector and project loans.

The "key problems" on which AID would focus its assistance were to be selected by the following criteria: those that were considered to be the most significant by governments in developing countries; those that were the most widespread among low-income countries; those that could be improved by assistance from external donors; those most relevant to AID's own policy objectives; and those considered relevant by a large number of USAID missions.

AID's efforts in development administration during the early 1970s concentrated on improving agricultural sector management, improving health services delivery management, and improving project planning and implementation systems.

Agricultural and Health Sector Management Systems

The agricultural management improvement projects were designed to help overcome what the AID staff perceived to be low levels of ability in the ministries of agriculture in less developed countries and "to provide the necessary kinds and amounts of essential inputs within the required time and at reasonable costs and risks." Thus, AID contracted with the Harvard Business School to design and test the management of a "seeds-to-consumer" commodity system for selected agricultural products. Harvard would help design the system, develop training materials and curricula and provide consulting and training services. The field studies and training were to be done primarily in Guatemala, Honduras, Nicaragua, and El Salvador in collaboration with the Central American Institute of Business Administration (INCAE).

A second project attempted to help developing countries implement agricultural plans and programs more effectively. Underlying the project was an assumption that in most countries agricultural development plans were too vague and abstract to be realistic or operational. A contract was signed with the Government Affairs Institute (GAI) in Washington to develop a conceptual framework and a process for "reducing the implementation deficiencies in agricultural development plans through designing such plans 'from the bottom up'. . . . through district, regional and national levels" (USAID, 1973: 1).

Underlying the project was a set of assumptions about the nature of the problem and the reasons why agricultural development plans were not effectively implemented (Waterston, 1973). First, it had been observed that in many developing countries agricultural development plans were inappropriate or unrealistic because capable planners were in short supply. Second, the lack of well-trained managers also accounted for the fact that plans, even if they had been realistic, could not be implemented effectively. Third, even when the plans were sound, they rarely indicated how they should be carried out, by whom, and when action was needed. Fourth, the plans were often not implemented because of inadequate communications and interaction among planners, technical ministries, local governments, and farmers. Finally, the gap between plan and performance was attributed to the lack of suitable administrative systems and organizational structures for managing complex agricultural and multisectoral rural development programs.

GAI would address these problems through five sets of activities (Waterston, 1973). It would assemble basic information about how to improve the formulation, implementation and management of plans, programs, and projects for agricultural and rural development; it would design a course of instruction to transfer the information to agricultural development managers in developing countries; and it would conduct seminars for trainers in selected institutions in developing countries. In addition, GAI would provide consultant services in creating, conducting, and following up on the training courses and disseminate the lessons of experience gained in carrying out the project to training institutes in developing countries.

GAI produced a comprehensive manual, *Managing Planned Agricultural Development,* which provided detailed information on linking agricultural and overall development planning, methods of preparing agricultural development plans, and potential objectives for an agricultural development program (Waterston, Weiss and Wilson, 1976). It offered instruction on "stocktaking and diagnostic surveys," on setting targets and allocating resources, on selecting agricultural strategies, and on choosing policy instruments. Moreover, it discussed methods of financing agricultural plans, designing and organizing development projects, providing extension, research, education, training, and consultant services. Finally, it covered methods of project and program control, monitoring, and evaluation.

The manual was a detailed reference book for those engaged in agricultural development project planning and program management, and a text that could be used in the training courses designed by GAI. Waterston and his associates prescribed new approaches to applied research and training. The research and training method was based on four principles. It prescribed an inductive rather than a deductive method of developing theory—that is, it drew together the lessons of experience in developing nations and then formulated theories to explain them. It compared theory and practice "to see what light practice throws on theory." It advocated learning from success—that is, it drew lessons primarily from projects and programs that seemed to have worked well rather than from those that had failed. Finally, it sought to explain *how* to achieve more successful projects, not merely to identify *what* must be done.

The training courses that emerged and that were tested initially in Washington, Nepal, and Egypt, and later in Ghana, Indonesia, and Jamaica used a "task-oriented" approach in which participants were asked to perform various tasks outlined in the manual—with the help of or coaching from the trainers—rather than a lecture or formal teaching approach. A crucial element of the training program was the "Coverdale Method," developed in England by the Coverdale management consulting group. The skill-building process involved: (1) setting group objectives; (2) using a systematic way of getting things done; (3) improving observation; (4) recognizing the strengths and skills of those involved in joint activities; (5) planning cooperation for mutual benefit; (6) learning to listen actively; and (7) recognizing how to apply management authority effectively.

Thus the training courses were designed not only to familiarize the participants with substantive knowledge about agricultural development planning, but also to teach them, through simulation experiences, about general managerial and organizational processes. In retrospect, the GAI trainers (Waterston, Weiss and Wilson, 1976; Annex G-6) found that

> while the task approach proved to be very successful for teaching purposes, what participants learned largely depended on how they viewed the opportunities presented by the tasks. At one extreme, a group would deal with a task as though it related to problems which might be encountered in the country of the group's participants. At the other extreme, another group used the same task to describe and justify the way its country dealt with problems raised in the task, without going beyond this to suggest improvements in the way problems were actually handled. One indication of the efficacy of the task as a learning device was the incidence of participant activity. There was an unusually low absence rate from PTC sessions. Failure to participate was rare.

Evaluations by participants indicated that the training did not provide them with the amount of management theory that they had anticipated. They complained that the issues dealt with during the course were limited to those raised in the training groups, and that the training programs were sometimes initially disorienting and discouraging. The training materials did not include issues pertaining to management in large organizations, and the courses did not provide the amount of technical training they expected. Others noted, however, that the Coverdale training techniques allowed them to learn by doing, to develop team-building and team-managing skills, to experiment with different personal and team roles, and to develop through repeated practice skills that could be applied to their work back at home.

Another set of projects initiated by AID's Office of Development Administration addressed the problems of improving the implementation of health plans and programs. An analysis was to be done of the factors contributing to what AID considered to be the inadequate execution of plans and possible remedies. The analysis was to be followed by a series of workshops with appropriate regional institutions, the preparation of case studies to determine the causes of poor implementation, and the development of methods for assessing the managerial capacity of health agencies. Because of delays in obtaining funding and in organizing the project, however, it did not get underway until the mid-1970s and was not completed until 1980.

Sector-oriented Project Management Systems

Finally, AID began to address the question of how to improve project planning and management capacity for specific sectors. In 1973, AID contracted with The Graduate School of Management at Vanderbilt University to develop training materials on project management for developing countries. The training materials were to focus on implementation within the framework of a generic "project cycle," that is, the actions required from the initial stages of identifying potential projects for funding by AID or by national governments through their design, appraisal, approval, organization, management, completion, and evaluation. The Vanderbilt contract yielded seven sets of training materials on various aspects of the project cycle: project organization and organizing, planning processes for project management, managing the project environment, problem solving, management information systems, control and evaluation processes for project management, and choice and adaptation of technology in development projects.

Some research was also done on the differences in the project cycles of various international assistance organizations and on the problems encountered by aid agencies and developing country governments in planning and managing various phases of the cycle. Rondinelli and Radosevich (1974) derived from the management practices of AID, the World Bank, and the United Nations Development Program (UNDP) a generic project cycle through which nearly all proposals for international funding had to proceed. Rondinelli (1976, 1976a, 1977) found that when the formal requirements of each international funding institution were combined, they created a formidable set of planning and management requirements for developing countries that were seeking assistance from AID and other international agencies.

Moreover, the research indicated that serious managerial problems arose for both developing countries and the aid agencies in trying to meet these project planning and implementation requirements (Rondinelli, 1976b). Given the complexity of the project management cycles used by international funding institutions, Solomon (1974) pointed out the need to develop administrative capacity within developing countries to manage projects as an integrated system of activities. The project cycle was considered to be an important framework for effective management because the various elements were inextricably related. "A defect in any of the phases of the project can make the project unsuccessful," Solomon (1974: 2) noted. "Thus, decision-makers have to be interested in all aspects of the project cycle." Also, elements of the cycle had to be carefully coordinated because of the large number of people and organizations making decisions affecting the project. "One person or group may conceive the idea, perhaps in a sector study, another may investigate it and give it a rough formulation, a third may give it a more detailed study, a fourth may approve it, a fifth may give it more detailed form," he noted, " and finally, another group or person may take responsibility for carrying out the plans."

Moreover, there came from the research undertaken by the Vanderbilt team a strong consensus that project planning and implementation must be more closely integrated. Examination of the activities at various stages of the project cycle indicated that those who designed the projects often did so without an understanding or appreciation of the managerial implications, and that those who were ultimately responsible for managing the project often had not been involved in its design. Solomon (1974: 3) argued that "training for project management thus must cover the whole project cycle, even though for any given group, concentration on a particular phase may be justified."

Unfortunately, however, the Vanderbilt group's research on project management in the aid agencies and developing countries—which would have allowed it to adapt the training materials to needs and conditions in developing countries—remained separate from the development of the "learning packages." As a result, the training packages included, almost exclusively, material on project management procedures used in the United States by private corporations and by the defense industry that had little to do with the problems of project management in developing countries (USAID, 1975).

In a sense, the project management learning packages developed by the Vanderbilt project simply reflected the application of what Esman and Montgomery had earlier referred to as the "Point Four approach" of transferring U.S. business management methods and techniques to developing countries. AID's evaluations noted that the training materials did make conceptual advances in describing important elements of the project cycle that were used by international aid agencies and the ways in which various parts of the cycle related to each other. They emphasized the differences in management problems among developing countries, project organizers, beneficiaries, and lending institutions. They highlighted the need for a multidisciplinary analysis of projects, and introduced new skills for project management, including creative problem solving, environmental assessment, and technology evaluation. But, when they were completed, their applicability in developing nations was limited.

Among the weaknesses of the training packages were that they simply were not practical for building the skills of managers in less developed countries because they were too theoretical. They drew primarily on U.S. corporate experience, there was little emphasis on the economic and financial aspects of project feasibility, and the approach to project management was too general and did not relate to the problems and opportunities in specific sectors. As a result, they could only be used as general resource materials that would require a great deal of revision for training programs in developing countries (USAID, 1975: 31-32).

The research commissioned by AID, however, raised serious questions about the efficacy of its own project planning and management procedures and about their applicability in developing countries. Rondinelli (1976a: 314) argued, for example, that the formal design and analysis requirements reflected in the project cycles of international agencies—including AID's PBAR system—had become so complex that their application "is beyond the administrative capabilities of most developing nations, thus intensifying their dependence on foreign experts and consultants for project planning. Foreign standards and procedures are imposed on governments, often without sensitivity to local needs and constraints." Rondinelli (1976, 1977, 1979, 1983) found that the project cycles—although they provided reasonable iterative models for planning and analyzing the actions that had to be taken in order for projects to be implemented—had become too rigid, inflexible, and complex to be managed by governments in developing countries. He called for the formulation of simpler, and more relevant and flexible procedures that could be used indigenously with the limited administrative capacity available in developing nations.

Many AID staff also found the systems management procedures stifling and inappropriate for the tasks of development. Judith Tendler, who had worked in USAID missions in Latin America, found that AID's technical procedures often discouraged or suppressed the creativity, innovativeness, and experimentation that were essential parts of promoting development. She argued that "the special character of the foreign aid agency's task requires that the organization have the proper atmosphere for groping without too much idea of what will result, for straying from tried and true solutions, and for struggling to escape from customary ways of thinking about things" (Tendler, 1975: 10). If AID was to be successful in tailoring projects to the conditions and needs of developing countries, the agency would need "a number of bureaucrats with a penchant for this type of behavior; and an organizational environment will have to exist to which such types are attracted, in which they can make cohesive and informal groups, and in which they are able to gain power." Instead, she found that the planning and management procedures in AID required standardization, compliance with rules and constraints, and detailed design of projects and programs without much concern for their appropriateness, or for the degree to which governments in developing countries were willing to support them. In short, the procedures created an atmosphere that was almost the opposite of that needed for AID staff to carry out their development tasks effectively.

Rondinelli (1974, 1976, 1979) suggested an approach to project design and implementation that would allow the agency to learn while doing, a concept that would later be reemphasized heavily in AID-sponsored research on development management. He suggested that AID projects be designed and implemented in such a way that planners and managers could learn more effectively about the conditions, needs, obstacles, and opportunities in the places where projects were to be carried out by proceeding incrementally through a series of smaller-scale activities. Where knowledge was weak and uncertainty was high, projects could be initially designed as small-scale experimental activities. When better information was available and innovative approaches to solving problems were devised, the projects could proceed to a pilot stage in which they would be tried under a wider variety of conditions. When pilot projects were proven successful, the results could be further tested and disseminated through demonstration projects. When the value and validity of the demonstrations were shown, AID could then proceed to the stage of replication or full-scale production and implementation. This incremental learning process for project planning and management would obviate the need to design projects comprehensively at the outset and would overcome many of the problems inherent in the complex and rigid management procedures that AID and other international assistance agencies had adopted.

To follow on from the work done by Vanderbilt and GAI, AID initiated in 1975 a set of technical assistance activities aimed at improving project management by building the capacity of four regional and four national training centers to offer project management training, consulting, "action research," and technical cooperation. The funds were to be used to help regional centers to adapt project management training materials developed by Vanderbilt and GAI to local needs and to test them under local conditions. Grants were also used to adapt the materials to particular sectors, such as health and agriculture. Among the regional centers that received grants were the Inter-American Institute for Development (EIAP), the Pan-African Institute for Development (PAID), the Inter-American Institute for Agricultural Sciences (IICA), and the Asian Institute of Management (AIM). The grants were used to develop training programs that covered the entire project cycle, as well as specific elements of project planning and management.

The project management systems and control procedures adopted by AID during the early 1970s, and prescribed for developing countries as a way of improving their administrative capacity, remained controversial for more than a decade and a half. Recurring criticism of their rigidity, inflexibility, and inappropriateness arose again during the late 1970s and early 1980s.

4

"New Directions" in Foreign Aid

Congressional criticism of the foreign assistance program continued throughout the early 1970s. The Nixon administration, realizing that foreign aid budgets would be cut in Congress, submitted in 1969 the lowest request for appropriations in the program's history, and complied with a Congressional requirement written into the 1968 foreign aid bill to undertake an extensive study "to reorganize and revitalize" U.S. economic assistance to developing countries. In the meantime, the Administration proposed that Congress create an Overseas Private Investment Corporation (OPIC) to take over the investment survey and promotion activities that had been carried out by AID. The administration also proposed that the foreign aid program give more emphasis to technical assistance programs providing training, research, institution building, and advisory services, and that provisions be made for the appointment of an AID auditor to monitor the use of foreign aid funds.

After taking office in 1969, Nixon appointed a task force headed by Rudolph A. Peterson, a former president of the Bank of America, to assess foreign aid programs and to suggest new directions for the 1970s. The Peterson committee recommended in 1970 a thorough revision of foreign aid, a proposal Nixon called "fresh and exciting" (CQS, 1969). Among the recommendations were that military and economic aid be separated administratively, with the Defense Department responsible for the former and the State Department responsible for the latter. The committee also suggested that two new organizations—a U.S. International Development Bank to administer the development loan program, and a U.S. International Development Institute to manage technical assistance programs—be created as independent government agencies to take over the functions performed by AID. An International Development Council composed of high-level government officials dealing with international economic policy would be established to coordinate aid activities and to formulate strategies. The Peterson committee suggested that the bulk of U.S. foreign assistance funds be channeled through international lending institutions such as the World Bank, the International Development Association, and the Inter-American Development Bank, all of which should receive higher contributions from the United States. The task force made a strong plea to Congress to increase U.S. economic assistance to developing countries.

In his foreign aid message to Congress in 1970, Nixon proposed most of the changes suggested by the Peterson committee. But, because of disputes over arms sales provisions of the military aid budget and debates over restrictions on aid to Vietnam and Cambodia, Congress did not take action on regular appropriations for foreign aid until the end of 1970, and little attention was given to organizational reforms.

By 1971, foreign aid programs were caught up in a bitter battle in the Senate over ending the Vietnam war, and Congress failed to complete action on the foreign aid budget. When a bill finally came before the Senate, both economic and military aid were rejected by a vote of 41-27. Both conservative and liberal senators criticized the program. Conservatives charged that the billions of dollars poured into developing countries by the United States failed to generate international support for U.S. foreign policies. Liberals argued that foreign aid had become dominated by military priorities and that it was no longer meeting its humanitarian purposes. Conservative Senator John L. McClellan of Arkansas charged that for too long the United States "has attempted to export democracy abroad to unwilling and unready recipients, while neglecting the obvious needs of our people and democratic institutions at home." He concluded that "foreign aid as an instrument of international diplomacy has been a flop and we should stop it." Liberal Senator Frank Church of Idaho told his colleagues that the foreign aid program had been "twisted into a parody and a farce." Church concluded that "the experience of twenty years of aid shows that we can neither bring about fundamental reform in tradition-encrusted societies nor prevent revolution in those countries where the tide of change runs deep and strong. . . . All we can do is to service the status quo in countries where it is not strongly challenged anyhow" (CQS, 1973: 877).

Unable to reconcile differences between Senate and House versions of the foreign assistance bills, congressional supporters of the aid program kept it alive only by "continuing resolutions" that allowed the Agency for International Development to spend money at previously approved budget levels. As the debates over foreign aid became more entangled in foreign policy issues, Congress was unable to agree on legislation extending the program in 1972, and AID's budget again was included in a continuing resolution that left funding at 1969 levels. Increasing demands were made by legislators in favor of economic assistance for fundamental reforms in the foreign aid program.

Political criticism of foreign aid was reinforced by increasing criticism of the economic growth theory that had been the basis of U.S. foreign assistance policy since the Marshall Plan. The criticism arose from mounting evidence that poverty in developing nations was becoming more widespread and serious, and the growing realization that problems in developing countries differed drastically from those faced by industrialized countries during their periods of economic development (Rondinelli, 1983). The debates over foreign aid brought about a fundamental rethinking of development policy in the early 1970s.

In a book that influenced the thinking of many of the members of AID's congressional oversight committees, Edgar Owens, an AID official, and Robert Shaw, a congressional staff member, argued that despite the outpouring of financial assistance over the previous twenty years and the rapid economic growth that occurred in many developing countries, the number of people living in poverty in the Third World was growing. "This expansion of poverty at the same time the countries are getting richer in GNP has created a nagging sense among the people of the United States that our humanitarian impulse has been misdirected. Not only has foreign aid appeared to be a way of involving and then entangling our country in situations that deteriorate into violence, but foreign aid dollars have also often seemed to increase the gap between rich and poor" (Owens and Shaw, 1972: 2). They emphasized that "somehow our assistance does not seem to have reached the heart of the problem—unemployment, the exploding population, the growing wretchedness of the urban slums, illiteracy, malnutrition, and disease. And if our foreign aid is strengthening policies that are destabilizing, then much of the criticism is justified."

Owens and Shaw concisely summarized the thinking of many scholars and practitioners who were involved in development assistance that the economic aid programs of the United States and of multilateral organizations had to be refocused on promoting social change, as well as economic growth in developing countries. The program had to be redesigned to assure that aid funds went to the people who really needed assistance rather than to reinforcing the power of existing regimes, or simply to making life more comfortable for the economic and political elite who ruled many developing countries. They called for reforms that would create in developing countries "a set of institutions which would give the underpriviliged person in the poor countries an opportunity to participate in the decisions most important to his life and which, furthermore, would link him to the mainstream of modern society." They insisted that by mobilizing local resources and energies, "the poor can be encouraged to invest more in their own futures, to raise their incomes through higher production, and have a greater say in the distribution of that production."

Heeding much of this advice, the House Foreign Affairs Committee took an active role in redesigning the foreign aid program. The Foreign Assistance Act of 1973 that emerged from the House and Senate foreign affairs committees was hailed as a new mandate for the administration and for AID. Its congressional authors saw it as a set of "new directions" for U.S. foreign assistance.

In the Foreign Assistance Act of 1973, Congress declared that the conditions under which foreign aid had been provided in the past had changed and that, in the future, aid policy would have to reflect the "new realities." Although U.S. aid had generally been successful in stimulating economic growth and industrial output in many countries, the House Committee on Foreign Affairs lamented that the gains "have not been adequately or equitably distributed to the poor majority in those countries," and that massive social and economic problems prevented the large majority of people from breaking out of the "vicious cycle of poverty which plagues most developing countries" (*U.S. Code Congressional and Administrative News*, 1973: 2811).

The Senate Foreign Relations Committee report on the bill emphasized that the new approach being proposed recognized that "economic growth alone does not necessarily lead to social advancement by the poor. Thus our policies and programs must be aimed directly at the poor majority's most pervasive problems" (U.S. Congress, 1973: 8). Congress instructed AID to give highest priority to activities in developing nations that "directly improve the lives of the poorest of their people and their capacity to participate in the development of their countries." The Foreign Assistance Act of 1973 set new guidelines for economic development assistance. Congress insisted that:

1. Bilateral development aid should concentrate increasingly on sharing American technical expertise, farm commodities, and industrial goods to meet critical development problems, and less on

large-scale capital transfers, which when made should be associated with contributions from other industrial countries working together in a multilateral framework.

2. United States assistance should concentrate on the development of labor-intensive technologies suitable to the less developed countries.

3. Future United States bilateral support for development should focus on critical problems in those functional sectors which affect the lives of the majority of people in the developing countries: food production, rural development and nutrition; population planning and health; education, public administration, and human resource development.

4. United States cooperation in development should be carried out to the maximum extent possible through the private sector; including those public service institutions which already have ties in the developing countries, such as educational institutions, cooperatives, credit unions, and voluntary agencies.

5. Development planning must be the responsibility of each sovereign country. United States assistance should be administered in a collaborative style to support the development goals chosen by each country receiving assistance.

6. United States bilateral development assistance should give the highest priority to undertakings submitted by host governments which directly improve the lives of the poorest of their people and their capacity to participate in the development of their countries.

Congress rejected the reorganization recommendations of the Peterson committee. Under the policy guidance of the secretary of state, the Agency for International Development was assigned the responsibility for coordinating all U.S. development assistance.

Not all critics of the foreign aid program were swayed from their opposition by the "new directions" mandate. The Foreign Assistance Act of 1973 was reported out of the Senate Foreign Relations Committee, for example, over the opposition of the committee chairman, Senator J. William Fulbright of Arkansas. In additional views attached to the Senate committee report on the bill, Fulbright called the bill "a face-lifting job for a badly sagging bilateral foreign aid program." He insisted that the claims of the bill's authors that they had set the foreign aid program in new directions were "both deceptive and defective." Fulbright argued that "the aid program will not be changed by this bill; even the authorization labels are the same as those in the AID congressional presentation book. The people who will administer the program will be the same as now. And they will be dispensing $1.2 billion for the same projects and programs AID has supported in the past. This is hardly the vigorous new initiative claimed for this measure by its principal sponsor" (U.S. Congress, 1973: 63).

But for the first time, Congress clearly identified AID's primary beneficiaries. Congress declared it the purpose of U.S. foreign assistance to alleviate the problems of the "poor majority" in developing nations. The new aid program would give less emphasis to maximizing national output and pursue what the House Foreign Affairs Committee called a "people-oriented problem-solving form of assistance." In its report accompanying the Foreign Assistance Act of 1973, the Foreign Affairs Committee argued that "we are learning that if the poorest majority can participate in development by having productive work and access to basic education, health care and adequate diets, then increased economic growth and social justice can go hand in hand."

In response to the "new directions" mandate, AID focused its programs and projects primarily on rural areas, where studies had shown that the vast majority of the poorest people in developing societies lived. It defined the primary "target groups" of U.S. assistance to be subsistence farm families, small-scale commercial farmers, landless farm laborers, pastoralists, unemployed laborers in market towns, and small-scale nonfarm entrepreneurs. The AID program would help the rural poor to increase their productivity and income. It would extend access to services and facilities to rural families that had previously been excluded from participation in productive economic activities (USAID, 1975b).

The "new directions" legislation also explicitly recognized that "the degree to which human talent, capital, and technology are successfully combined to achieve development goals and improve people's lives depends on management skills," and that these skills were weak in nearly all in developing countries (U.S. Congress, 1973: 13). Thus, the Foreign Assistance Act of 1973 reaffirmed that help "will be provided through the foreign aid program in the general field of public admistration."

The Local Action Approach to Development Administration

From the early years of the U.S. foreign aid program, and perhaps manifested most clearly in the community development movement, many aid professionals believed that local organizations and local governments played a crucial role in economic and social development. Although community development as an administrative approach had been largely abandoned by AID in the 1960s, the interest in working through local groups was still strong among many development professionals.

In the early 1970s, AID's Asia Bureau commissioned a series of studies by Cornell University's Rural Development Committee of the role of local organizations in rural development. Case studies in sixteen countries indicated that local governments did indeed play a crucial role in the development process and in providing the possibility for people to participate in it. Among the functions that local governments performed were planning for and administering some national services and facilities at the local level; providing small-scale infrastructure and services in rural areas; budgeting and allocating local and national revenues for municipal operating expenses and small capital investments; and collecting local taxes, levies, and other revenues. In some countries, local governments played an active role in arbitrating local conflicts, processing claims, channeling the requests and demands of local groups to higher levels of government, and managing small local and provincial projects. Local governments in some countries also provided a communications link between national and provincial governments and private organizations and assisted local communities with self-help projects.

Local organizations such as cooperatives, mutual benefit and social organizations, and political parties, it was found, also played important roles in rural development by assisting with the delivery of productive and social services, mobilizing local resources, organizing cooperative and self-help activities, and acting as intermediaries between government officials and local residents (Uphoff and Esman, 1974).

Comparing experience in the sixteen countries that the Cornell group had studied, Uphoff and Esman (1974: xi) argued that the cases showed "a strong, empirical basis for concluding that local organization is a necessary if not sufficient condition for accelerated rural development, especially development which emphasizes improvement in the productivity and welfare of the majority of rural people."

A major finding of the studies was that if AID wanted to strengthen local organizations as a means of implementing development projects or of promoting popular participation in them, it would have to provide assistance to strengthen a *system* of local organizations in an area rather than simply building the capacity of a single institution. Uphoff and Esman (1974) found no case in which a single organization was responsible for rural development or where linkages and interactions among local organizations were not crucial for development. If rural insitutions were to play a strong role in development, they had to be linked into a larger organizational network.

They found that in both mixed economies and socialist societies in Asia, rural programs were the responsibility of a mixture of local, provincial, and national governments and of political and private organizations. The complementarities among them were as important to the success of rural development as the functions performed by any particular organization. "While there are isolated instances of local organization taking the initiative, mobilizing resources and accomplishing certain development objectives, in most countries considered, the cumulative effect of such efforts has been negligible," Uphoff and Esman (1974: xi) reported. "What count are systems or networks of organization, both vertically and horizontally, that make local development more than an enclave phenomenon." It was these networks of local organizations that AID would have to help strengthen.

Local Action in Rural Development

AID's interest in local organizations was revitalized by the new orientation of the Foreign Assistance Act of 1973 toward the poor and rural areas. In 1974, as a result of the "new directions" mandate, AID began to explore the factors affecting the successful planning and implementation of projects that were aimed at helping small-scale farmers. AID contracted with a consulting firm, Development Alternatives Incorporated (DAI), to carry out the applied research. The purpose of the project was "to assist AID in understanding how more successfully to work with the rural poor" and to conform more effectively to new congresssional directives to AID (Morton, 1979).

The study included field visits to eighty-one technical assistance projects in African and Latin American countries. The results, published in a two-volume report, *Strategies for Small Farmer Development: An Empirical Study of Rural Development Projects* (Morss, Hatch, Mickelwait, and Sweet, 1975), indicated that of the twenty-five major factors that distinguished relatively successful from less successful rural development projects, two accounted for about 49 percent of the variation. These were, first, the degree of involvement of small farmers themselves in the process of decision making during the implementation of the projects and, second, the degree to which farmers were required and willingly agreed to commit their own resources—usually labor and money—to completing the projects.

The combination of these two factors was defined as *local action*, a necessary but not sufficient condition for the success of rural development projects. The study found, moreover, that three variables were positively associated with the level of local action: first, the specificity of the agricultural information offered by extension services to smallholders; second, the existence of effective local organizations; and third, the creation of an effective two-way communications flow between the project staff and participating farmers.

DAI's studies strongly confirmed the conclusions of Cornell's research about the importance of local organizations. DAI's field evaluations found that some of AID's most successful agricultural development projects in Africa and Latin America had been those that worked through indigenous local organizations and practices. It was found that indigenous social and economic institutions, no matter how inadequate they seemed to be for promoting modernization to outside technical assistance experts, survived because they performed necessary functions. They were often well adapted to local cultural conditions and they satisified local needs. Fishing village projects in Ghana and vegetable production schemes in Gambia gradually increased productivity and income, for instance, only by organizing communal labor through traditional arrangements and by incorporating the customary roles of women in agricultural decision making. Some of AID's agricultural projects in Bolivia succeeded by adapting a variation of traditional sharecropping methods in which it was necessary for the patron to finance all cash costs and then share the crops with the farmers. Capital accumulation was promoted through AID projects for the Tiv tribes in Nigeria through the use of "bams," farmers' associations that had been formed to lend food and money to participating families in emergencies. The studies found that although traditional borrowing practices would not generate sufficient savings to purchase farm equipment and fertilizer, they could only introduce more modern savings and lending functions by organizing them around traditional food-lending groups and transforming them, over time, into more diversified farmers' associations.

Working through local organizations and arrangements was essential for projects to have a beneficial impact on small-scale farmers, but other factors were also important. Either the project had to provide—or other institutions had to offer—an adequate technological package for agricultural improvements, timely delivery of needed agricultural inputs, and effective extension services. In addition, there had to be favorable markets for agricultural produce and the means for farmers to get their goods to market. This combination of factors created a set of conditions that would allow AID projects more successfully to meet the needs of poor farmers in developing countries. Indeed, the case studies indicated that projects were most relevant and elicited the greatest participation when they were designed and managed in such a way that the geographical boundaries of the projects were well-defined and the client population was easily identifiable (Morss et al., 1975: 95-96). In successful projects, the staff actively sought the participation of local leaders and farmers, or delegated to them control over decisions concerning project design and implementation. Farmers were usually involved jointly with the professional staff in testing technological packages and organizational arrangements to be used in the project.

Moreover, projects were more successful when participants were socially and economically homogeneous; when the project staff developed an effective communications process with and among local participants; organizational arrangements were created to give farmers a voice in decisions concerning project management; and when high priority was placed on technical training of participants, especially when farmers were used as paraprofessionals to teach others technical skills. Effective projects were those in which farmers' involvement was related initially to single-purpose activities such as credit provision or crop promotion, and later broadened. Systems of accountability were usually established in the more successful projects to permit changes in leadership among local participants and to ensure that services were provided efficiently. Finally, projects were implemented more effectively when opportunities were offered for local organizations to participate initially in income-generating activities.

The studies concluded that if projects were designed by these principles, they would not only deliver services more effectively, but also build the capacity of farmers to help themselves and sustain the benefits after the projects were completed.

Toward a Process Approach to Project Management

More broadly, the studies again questioned the effectiveness of the PBAR project planning procedures that AID had adopted in the early 1970s and in which heavy emphasis was placed on detailed and thorough design of the project prior to committing funds and signing an agreement with the government. Referring to AID's standardized and somewhat rigid project design procedures as a "blueprint" approach, DAI's analysts noted that the large gap between design and implementation, which was referred to frequently in AID's own evaluation reports, was due to the fact that effective rural development simply could not be designed in detail in advance and be standardized for all developing countries, or even for different areas of the same country. "Unfortunately, it is impossible to specify precisely what is needed, when it should be provided, and by whom without a detailed knowledge of local conditions," Morss and his associates argued (1975: 319).

The report concluded that instead of attempting to design a project in detail at the outset, AID should use a process approach. "Our study suggests that the most successful projects are those which have attempted to gain a knowledge of the local area prior to project initiation or have structured the project in such a way as to start with a simple idea and to develop this required knowledge base during the initial project stages," Morss and his associates reported. The process should occur mainly by collecting adequate information during the early stages of the project, involving beneficiaries in design and implementation, and redesigning the project when necessary during implementation.

The data collected prior to designing the project was most crucial and should include information that would help in understanding and overcoming constraints imposed on small farmers by the local environment. AID had to ensure that project components were adequate, and had to find ways of providing needed services and knowledge. A great deal of attention had to be given to determining the proper focus for the project and the organizational capabilities within the area so that small-scale farmers would actually receive the benefits.

In sum, sufficient data about local conditions were needed to better define the behavioral changes required by small farmers and to design the project to bring those changes about. More important, however, DAI's studies underlined the need for flexibility in modifying project designs during implementation rather than viewing deviations from the original plans ("blueprints") as managerial problems or as indicators of poor performance. "Few projects can survive a rigid blueprint which fixes at the time of implementation the development approaches, priorities and mechanisms for achieving success," Morss and his associates argued (1975: 329-330). "Most projects scoring high on success experienced at least one major revision after the project [managers] determined that the original plan was not working. This flexibility is critical, particularly if the technology is uncertain and if the local constraints facing the small farmers are not well known." The study concluded that revisions of project designs during their implementation should be viewed as desirable if assistance aimed at improving the conditions of the small-scale farmers and other groups of the rural poor was to be more successful.

The Hall Committee Report and Changes in
Development Management Strategy

AID's activities in the field of project and program management were influenced during the 1970s by an agency-wide assessment of technical assistance for development management conducted in 1974 and 1975. The AID Work Group on Management and Development Administration, headed by Ambassador William O. Hall, reviewed the agency's experience and made recommendations for improvement (USAID, 1975a: 2-5). The committee reemphasized that AID's management assistance activities should be focused on improving program and project implementation in its high-priority sectors—food production, rural development, nutrition, population planning, health, and education and human resources. These sectors were thought to provide the greatest benefits for the majority of people in developing countries, and especially for the agency's new target group—the poor. In each sector, management assistance should be focused on "results-" and "service-oriented" planning and management in collaboration with host governments. The management assistance provided by AID should emerge from the identification by governments in developing countries of their needs to improve management capacity to deliver services. It should help to build the capacity of government and private organizations to deliver services that people need and want.

The Hall task force insisted that the management assistance methods used by AID in developing countries "must be applied flexibly, with experimentation to learn while doing, take advantage of opportunities, and move from pilot projects to large-scale efforts." The committee also recommended that procedures and criteria be developed to allow AID to appraise and assess the management capacity of developing countries early in the project cycle—at the stage when projects were first identified and in their initial design. These criteria would allow the agency to determine whether or not governments in developing countries had the managerial capability to carry out a particular project and, if not, to identify the managerial assistance they would need to implement successfully high-priority projects that were considered to be economically and technically feasible.

The Hall committee suggested that AID engage in more extensive applied research into the managerial problems and needs of developing countries in the agency's high-priority sectors so that AID could formulate and offer more appropriate and relevant management assistance. The task force urged AID to induce its contractors and the research institutes in developing countries that it funded to concern themselves more directly with the management of service delivery, the use of services, and their distribution among beneficiaries, as well as with technical and scientific problems. Sectoral management training programs, the committee emphasized, should be offered by AID to key institutions in the countries that had the greatest capacity to adapt and disseminate them, and should focus on building up the ability of institutions in developing countries to do their own managerial analysis, training, and evaluation. Finally, the committee suggested that AID increase the resources for development administration assistance, applied research on sectoral management problems, experimentation and testing of new management techniques, and consultative services to USAID missions and host country governments. Most of these recommendations were later incorporated into AID's official "Policy Determination on Development Administration," issued by the administrator, Daniel Parker, in 1977 (USAID, 1977). Parker noted that "it is AID policy to assure the existence or development of competent management in the specific host-country institutions responsible for carrying out AID-financed programs and projects to assure with reasonable certainty their successful completion." Management improvement, the administrator argued, "deserves attention equal with that afforded the economic, technical, political and social dimensions of development."

Assessing Managerial Capacity

One immediate result of the Hall committee's recommendations was to set AID's Office of Development Administration the task of formulating guidelines for the appraisal of project management capacity in developing nations. The guidelines defined appraisal of managerial capacity as the assessment of "the managerial strengths and weaknesses of recipient's leading implementing organizations. Appraisal results are then incorporated into project design and development and proposed corrective action" (Rizzo and Koteen, 1976: 14). *Project management capacity* was defined as the recipient organizations' ability to implement projects, which was "greatly affected by the way they are organized and led, by the way they plan and control their work, by the way they mobilize and manage their resources [money, manpower, supplies and facilities], and by the environment in which they operate."

The guidelines suggested that an assessment of managerial capacity take place at various stages of the project cycle. At the stage of project identification, USAID missions should describe in the project identification document significant managerial problems that might arise in implementing proposed activities and the range of responses that AID could expect from the government in resolving them. The PID should contain a brief discussion of administrative issues within the country that might affect the success of the project.

The report recommended that at the stage of initial design and review, USAID missions should include in their Project Review Papers (PRPs) a description of the agency in the developing country that would implement the project, an initial assessment of its capability, and a description of major deficiencies and problems that would affect the success of the project. At the stage of detailed design and appraisal, the missions should include in their Project Papers (PPs) an assessment of the implementing agency's managerial capability with regard to the following factors: (1) appropriateness of its role, (2) quality of leadership, (3) the degree to which the organizational setting was supportive, (4) the soundness of the organizational structure, (5) the effectiveness of planning and control, (6) the efficiency of resource administration, (7) the degree to which organizational behavior was constructive to the project's success, and (8) capacity for effective service delivery.

Perhaps the most important role of the report was that it provided AID staff with specific questions to ask and indicators to use in assessing managerial capacity, as well as for assessing the implementing agencies' financial management capability and the degree of administrative support the government was likely to provide during the implementation of the project. When deficiencies or weaknesses were found, the USAID missions were to recommend actions to increase the implementing agencies' managerial and administrative capacity. These actions could either be designed as part of the project itself, or be included in the conditions that the government would have to meet before receiving approval of funding, or as a condition for receiving financial disbursements. These guidelines were later incorporated into AID procedures for preparing PIDs and PPs.

Managing Participation in Development Projects

In the "new directions" mandate, Congress placed strong emphasis on the need for participation by local groups who would be influenced by, or for whom benefits were intended from, AID-sponsored development projects and programs. From the late 1960s on, there had been a growing consensus in AID that popular participation in development activities was a necessary condition for success. Indeed, in the late

1960s, Congress had added Title IX to the Foreign Assistance Act of 1961 that required AID to place emphasis "on assuring maximum participation in the task of economic development on the part of the people of developing countries, through the encouragement of democratic local government institutions."

The "new directions" mandate in the Foreign Assistance Act of 1973 focused even more strongly on the need for participation by the poor in development projects and programs. Yet there was little consensus within AID on what participation meant—different groups within the agency defined it differently—or on the most effective means of eliciting it. Thus, in 1977, AID commissioned a study from Cornell University of ways of analyzing the potential for participation in project design and implementation. It also entered into a cooperative agreement with Cornell to provide technical assistance to "participatory projects" in developing countries.

Cornell researchers undertook extensive studies of projects in which the managers were attempting to elicit participation or where participation was a crucial variable in successful development activities. Field studies were done of AID projects and programs in Botswana, Jamaica, the Philippines, Nepal, Tanzania, Sri Lanka, India and other countries.

In its applied research studies, the Cornell team attempted to develop a framework for analyzing participation and to define more clearly its meaning and characteristics. In the team's final report, Uphoff, Cohen and Goldsmith (1979: 4) argued that

> asking "What is participation?" may be the wrong question, since it implies that participation is a single phenomenon. It appears more fruitful and proper to regard participation as a descriptive term denoting *the involvement of a significant number of persons in situations or actions which enhance their well-being, e.g., their income, security or self-esteem. . . .* We find it more instructive, however, to think in terms of *three dimensions of participation:* (1) *what* kind of participation is under consideration? (2) *who* is participating in it? and (3) *how* is participation occurring?

The framework attempted to address these and other questions that project designers and managers might ask in considering how to increase participation. Four types of participation were identified: participation in *decision making,* in *implementation,* in *benefits,* and in *evaluation.* Also, four sets of potential participants in rural development projects and programs were identified—local residents, local leaders, government personnel, and foreign personnel—each often having different perceptions, interests, and definitions of a project's benefits. Means of identifying how participation was occurring were also described—the types of initiatives that were used to elicit participation (mobilized from the center or autonomous); the types of inducements for participation (voluntary or coercive); the structure and channels of participation (individual or collective, formal or informal, direct or representative); the duration (intermittent or continuous) and scope (narrow or broad range of activities); and the results of participation (whether or not it leads to "empowerment"—that is, increases the capacity of people to satisfy their objectives and needs through involvement).

The framework identified the contextual characteristics that define the ability of various groups to be involved in projects. These contextual characteristics included: technological complexity, resource requirements, tangibility of benefits, probability of benefits occurring, the immediacy of benefits, equity, program linkages, program flexibility, administrative flexibility, and administrative coverage.

Finally, the framework encompassed a set of environmental factors that create opportunities and constraints for participation—the physical, biological, economic, political, social, cultural and historical conditions of the area in which the project would be carried out.

The output of the research remained somewhat abstract, and a later assessment pointed out that "ultimately, the Cornell project on rural development may be less important for the specific programmatic guidelines it has produced than for its positive role in familiarizing field practitioners with the importance of participation and advocating it as a central aspect of any rural development project. In so doing, the Cornell researchers have given the elusive concept of participation a concrete and relevant definition for field practitioners" (Cohen, Grindle, and Thomas, 1983: 78-79).

Organization and Administration of Integrated Rural Development Project

The strong influence of the "new directions" mandate in focusing the agency's attention on the problems of the poor, and especially on those of the marginal and subsistence groups in rural areas, also led AID in 1978 to sponsor a large research and technical assistance project on the administration and organization of integrated rural development projects. The objective was "to increase the effectiveness of on-going Integrated Rural Development (IRD) projects and to improve the design and management of future rural development efforts which combine social services, income production, and production-support functions in a single project" (USAID, 1978).

In addition to providing technical assistance to more than a dozen AID-sponsored integrated rural development projects, the contractors—Development Alternatives Incorporated (DAI)—also produced a study of the management and organization of multisectoral rural development activities (Honadle, Morss, Van Sant and Gow, 1980). The study found a number of common and frequently recurring problems in the management of such projects, including difficulties in integrating and coordinating the activities of the many participating government agencies required to provide agricultural, social and productive services; difficulties in managing and supervising teams of multidisciplinary technical and administrative staff needed to carry out the projects; inadequate information needed to make effective managerial decisions; and the lack of incentives for project staff or personnel from cooperating organizations to act in ways that effectively support the objectives of integrated rural development projects. Other problems included frequent difficulties in procuring supplies, equipment, and personnel in a timely manner to carry out the project on schedule, resulting in delays and cost overruns and the diversion of resources intended for integrated rural development projects to other purposes and uses. Inappropriate use of technical assistance, ineffective use of project outputs by intended beneficiaries, and the failure to sustain project activities or outputs when foreign assistance or domestic aid for the project ended also undermined its implementation.

The studies revealed the importance of proper organizational structure in the successful implementation of integrated rural development projects and, indeed, in any multisectoral development program. Proper organizational design, DAI analysts found, included choosing the most effective organizational *level* at which to locate the project to assure the integration of decisions and resources, the appropriate *institution* to manage the projects, and the best configuration of internal organizational *divisions*. Four major organizational arrangements were being used for integrated rural development projects: national line agencies, subnational units of government, integrated development authorities, and project management units—each of which had advantages and disadvantages, and each of which required the existence of specific conditions to allow them to operate effectively (DAI, 1980).

National line agencies, such as ministries of agriculture, provided projects with a base in a permanent institution, could involve top-level decision makers in project activities, were sometimes appropriate for projects that were not focused on a particular geographical area of the country, and often simplified initial project preparation processes and strengthened the flow of resources to the project. However, national line agencies usually perceived the project from their own sectoral focus, and were often preoccupied with national rather than local problems. They were usually unwilling to delegate operational authority to project managers or to local organizations, and were often involved in conflicts with other national agencies. All of these weaknesses could undermine the effectiveness of project implementation. In order for national line agencies to manage projects effectively they had to have a high level of management capacity, strong political commitment, and good relations with the intended beneficiaries. They were most appropriate for managing projects that required a strong institutional base in order to survive.

Implementation by a subnational government organization such as a regional, provincial, or district unit had the advantage of providing a local perspective and reacting quickly to local problems. They allowed authority over project activities to be concentrated at the level of implementation, and their administrative and planning capabilities could be strengthened through the experience of carrying out IRD projects. However, subnational government organizations often had few financial resources or highly skilled administrators. They were usually weak institutions with little influence with the line ministries that provided resources or whose activities affected local projects. Implementation by subnational units of government was most often appropriate when a project had to be decentralized in order to meet its goals or when the area in which the project was to be carried out had unique characteristics that required local management. Subnational organizations that had unusually high levels of management capability or strong relationships with the beneficiary group were more successful in implementing IRD projects.

National integrated development agencies that were responsible for a wide variety of functions rather than just for particular sectoral activities such as transportation, public works, or agriculture had the advantage of being free from some of the rigid audit and control procedures imposed on regular line agencies. They could provide local interest groups with access to national agencies, and they could provide a more comprehensive perspective on how the project could be implemented. However, many such agencies competed with line ministries for resources and power, and their conflicts could cripple a project's implementation. Moreover, in order to obtain resources, coordinate their activities, and sustain political support, all of which were difficult to do in developing countries, integrated development agencies had to maintain complex lines of communication. These authorities were most appropriate for implementing projects that depended on technologies that would fail unless complementary inputs were provided expeditiously.

Finally, autonomous project management units established temporarily to implement IRD projects were found to be strong in concentrating authority within a single organization to carry out the project and in avoiding many of the stringent financial, personnel, and procurement constraints on regular line agencies. But it was found that almost everywhere they were used, their temporary nature created serious personnel managment problems and difficulties in sustaining the outputs of the project after international funding ended. They were most appropriate for projects that used highly uncertain technology, that had the task of providing relatively simple infrastructure, or that would be adversely affected by the cumbersome administrative procedures usually found in governments in developing countries.

DAI's consultants studied IRD projects that were organized both at the central government level and at regional and local levels of administration. But they found no universally applicable lessons about the potential advantages of centralization over decentralization. They determined that each had strengths and weaknesses that must be assessed carefully in each country before organizational choices were made.

The difficulties of managing and supervising the staff of integrated rural development projects were due to the fact that those who were assigned as managers of IRD projects were usually successful technicians—engineers, agronomists, or extension agents—who had little or no general management experience or training.

The researchers found that IRD projects could be more effectively managed if they were designed, not in AID's conventional "blueprint" fashion, but through a learning process in which:

1. The design is done in discrete phases rather than in great detail prior to the project's approval.
2. A large amount of short-term technical assistance is provided to help the staff deal with particular technical problems as they arise.
3. Emphasis is placed on action-oriented, problem-related, field training of both staff and beneficiaries,
4. Rewards and incentives are provided to the staff to carry out project activities effectively and that are consistent with a learning and performance orientation.
5. Applied research is made a part of the project so that staff can test and learn from new ideas.
6. Simple, field-level information systems are used that collect new information only after an inventory has been made of existing data, identify the information that decision makers are currently using, determine how the information will be

used, and assess the costs of information collection and analysis.

7. Provisions are made for redesign of the project—its objectives, organization, procedures, and staffing needs—as managers learn more about its operation and effectiveness during implementation.

The studies noted that the impact of IRD projects was often limited because the intended beneficiaries had not participated in their design and implementation. Planners often ignored or underestimated the target group's perception of risk in participating in rural development projects that were uncertain or untried. Unsuccessful projects were also found to be administratively and technically complex. Often, the results that the projects were designed to achieve were those more important to the international assistance agencies than to local groups.

A number of organizational and managerial attributes were found to be essential to assuring better results for intended beneficiaries. These included openness to participation by a broad range of community groups, ability to adapt activities to culturally accepted practices, capacity to perform multiple functions, the ability to establish and maintain strong linkages with other organizations on which resources and political support depended, and the willingness and ability to distribute benefits equitably.

Local participation could be enhanced, these studies indicated, if organizations responsible for integrated development projects adapted new ideas to local circumstances and conditions, devised ways of gaining acceptance for new ideas among the intended beneficiaries, obtained a commitment of resources from the beneficiaries, limited or reduced exploitation of the groups they were working with, and designed projects in such a way that they could be handed over to the beneficiary groups for implementation when foreign assistance ended.

Moreover, the response of local groups to integrated rural development projects could be improved if the projects were organized and managed to be responsive to the needs of intended beneficiaries, developed and used a local base of social support, and developed local leadership and control.

The studies suggested that integrated rural development projects should be kept small in size. They should focus on overcoming critical constraints to rural development in the areas in which they are located, and should be designed to build up gradually the organizational capacity of beneficiary groups so that they could participate in, and eventually control, project activities.

Managing Benefits Through Targetted Projects

Both the "new directions" mandate and the concern expressed in the Hall committee report for assuring that AID's programs and projects were designed and managed in a way that would allow benefits to flow to the poor majority, led the agency in 1979 to commission a study of the management of "aid-targeting." In the study, *Managing Benefits for the Poor,* Ingle, Rondinelli, and Riley (1981) noted the difficulty that both the agency's technical offices in Washington and the USAID missions often had in designing and managing projects to assure that the poor actually received the benefits of development activities, and that the aid program in each country was adequately addressed to the needs of the poor majority.

In response to a Congressional inquiry in 1975 about AID's progress in carrying out the "new directions" mandate, agency officials frankly acknowledged the difficulties of defining poverty and distinguishing among different groups of the poor in developing countries. AID staff (USAID, 1975b: 5) told Congress that "few officials in developed or developing countries have spent time on that question, perhaps feeling that 'you know the poor when you see them,' and that attention could more usefully go to designing and implementing programs for people who are obviously poor by any reasonable standards."

In its agency-wide programming, AID chose to define the poor in developing countries by a rough set of "benchmarks," consisting of data on per capita income, dietary and nutritional levels, and social indicators such as life expectancy, infant mortality, birth rates, and access to basic health services. By these criteria, AID estimated that about 75 percent of the population—or about 800 million people—in AID-assisted developing countries were living in poverty in 1975.

Although these benchmarks provided some indication of the magnitude of poverty, AID officials recognized that relatively little could be done with the resources available to the agency to bring the majority of the poor close to or above the benchmark levels. AID officials pointed out in their report to Congress that "while AID-financed programs must attempt to reach large numbers of poor people, AID's primary target group will often be a limited portion of the majority in each country depending on its economic and social conditions, its capabilities and desires, and other considerations which determine the programs yielding the most impressive benefits at the least cost" (USAID, 1975b: 6).

USAID missions continued to express frustration throughout the late 1970s about the difficulty of targeting aid effectively for the poor. The Philippines mission, for example, which had developed one of the most comprehensive analyses of poverty, still complained that "poverty is an elusive concept. Many definitions and measures have been advanced. All have limitations in methodology and applicability to specific country conditions" (USAID, 1980: 1). Officials in AID's Pakistan mission pointed out that "virtually no conceptual framework exists to develop an operational poverty definition rooted in established social values" (USAID, 1979: 4). The difficulties of defining and distinguishing among groups of the poor were reflected in the fact that many AID project proposals simply begged the question; they were justified by language that seemed to address the needs of the poor in general without specifying exactly which groups would benefit from proposed projects and programs.

Thus, AID's Office of Development Administration sought through a review of mission strategies, project proposals, and evaluations to identify more clearly the constituent groups of the poor for whom projects were designed. It wanted to determine which approaches that missions were using to channel benefits to the poor could be used by others having difficulties with aid-targeting, the management factors affecting aid-targeting, and implications for improving targeting in AID policies, programs, and projects.

Ingle, Rondinelli, and Riley (1981) found that a few USAID missions had been more successful than others in identifying constituent groups of the poor, in defining the benefits that projects would provide to them, and in developing mechanisms for delivering benefits effectively. Among the constituent groups most often identified were: (1) poor rural smallholders, subsistence farmers, pastoralists, and minority groups with low levels of social welfare; (2) low-income urban residents and recent rural migrants to cities; (3) landless laborers; (4) women with low levels of literacy, nutrition, and health; (5) people living in rural areas and regions with particularly underdeveloped economies; and (6) groups of ethnic minorities that had previously been excluded from programs of economic and social development.

A number of USAID missions had also attempted to identify the causes of poverty. Among the major ones identified were national economic policies that were adverse to widespread economic growth or to the equitable distribution of benefits, inadequate agricultural resources or lack of access for the poor to productive assets, and poor natural resource bases in some areas of the country. Moreover, other missions found instances where social and political practices discriminated against large groups of people or against particular areas of the country, where the national government was simply not committed to equitable distribution of the benefits of development, or where weak administrative and institutional structures prevented benefits from being distributed widely. Still others identified the characteristics of areas or groups themselves that seemed to account for their poverty such as lack of access to transportation and infrastructure, lack of access to appropriate technology, limited management capabilities, lack of access to jobs, capital, or social services, inability to participate in development activities, and lack of education and skills.

Finally, Ingle, Rondinelli, and Riley (1981) identified the major mechanisms that some USAID missions were able to devise, and that others might be able to adapt, for distributing the benefits of development more equitably to AID's target groups. These included ten major sets of mechanisms:

1. Policies to redistribute resources by taxation and investment allocation policies, the creation of government enterprises to promote redistribution of goods and services, and land reform
2. Policies to make income distribution more equitable through appropriate pricing policies, selective interventions in rural areas to raise income, and growth generating policies that made more income available to poorer households
3. Programs to influence short-term demand for productive assets or opportunities for poverty groups—including programs that lower the costs of providing services to the poor, disseminate information to poor households about employment opportunities, simplify methods of service delivery, help small-scale farmers better maintain infrastructure and equipment, and promote labor-intensive agricultural production processes to employ more of the rural poor
4. Programs for influencing long-term demand for productive assets or opportunities by poverty groups, such as promoting self-help activities that reduce the poor's dependence on the government for services and productive inputs
5. Projects to expand or extend the supply of existing opportunities to specific groups of the poor, e.g., market town development activities, provision of community health clinics and physicians, extension of rural works and infrastructure, and concentrating services and facilities in settlements that are easily accessible for the rural poor
6. Projects to increase the appropriateness of existing opportunities and to extend them to poor households, such as developing appropriate technology for production, increasing the numbers of rural extension workers, introducing production expanding technologies to low-yield agricultural areas and encouraging the location of labor-absorbing industries in poor communities or regions

7. Arrangements that involve the poor in decision making at various stages of the project cycle, such as eliciting the involvement of poor beneficiaries in project selection, stimulating local self-help activities, and involving the poor in project implementation to assure that the needs of the poor are met more effectively

8. Arrangements that better coordinate or integrate services for specific groups of the poor, for instance, integrated service delivery programs for particular communities or ethnic groups, and decentralization of program administration to assure that the needs of the poor are met by government agencies

9. Means of supplementing or increasing the administrative capacity of beneficiary groups to plan, assess, and manage their own development activities

10. Experiments on new approaches to extending the benefits of projects to constituent groups of the poor, such as funding regional demonstration projects, developing pilot and demonstration projects that can be replicated or extended by private and voluntary organizations, and providing more resources for experiments that seek to assist the poor

However, the study found that only a few USAID missions gave serious attention to trying to identify constituent groups of the poor effectively and to designing and managing projects in ways that would increase the probability that benefits would actually reach them. Moreover, even among the few missions that had given the problem serious attention, there were large gaps between their capacity to identify target groups, the causes of poverty, and means of distributing benefits on the one hand, and their ability to translate these analyses into effective project proposals on the other.

The study identified seven project management practices that would help Missions to target aid more effectively:

1. Specific poverty reduction objectives should be established and clearly stated by AID and other major participants in the project proposal.

2. Specific groups of the poor should be identified in the area where the project will be carried out and their needs and characteristics should be described in the project proposal.

3. The causes of poverty should be described and analyzed for each group of the poor whom the project is intended to benefit prior to its detailed design.

4. Intervention strategies should be identified to address the major causes of poverty, and the proportion and sequencing of

benefits from the project should be described in the project proposal.

5. The project proposal should describe the mechanisms or arrangements through which its benefits would be distributed to the intended beneficiaries.
6. The institutional arrangements through which the benefits would be distributed to the poor should be identified and analyzed prior to project approval.
7. The project proposal should describe the means by which the distribution of benefits to the poor would be monitored and evaluated during implementation and after completion of the project.

The study found that most USAID missions fell far short of applying these management practices in the design of development strategies, in the implementation of projects, in activities to assure the continuation of benefits when the projects were completed, and in project monitoring and evaluation. The report concluded that "program implementation is not yet a central feature of AID's agenda. Country Development Strategy Statements, project papers, and impact studies are concerned primarily with resource inputs and finances. There is scant discussion of what occurs between inputs and results. Implementation resembles a 'black box' known so well to psychologists. The issue of how mutual objectives are defined and translated into processes of successful implementation remains unexplored." The report emphasized that part of the problem "is that development administration in AID and elsewhere is a generation out of date. As practiced in AID, it is concerned with training, consulting, and administrative processes rather than with results-oriented management."

The study recommended a number of actions that AID technical offices in Washington could take to assist missions to design and manage projects in ways that would distribute their benefits to intended target groups more effectively. These included:

1. Developing a collaborative project design process through which major participants and intended beneficiaries could clarify and agree on the primary objectives of AID programs and projects
2. Identifying and disseminating cost-effective methods for gathering and analyzing socioeconomic data about specific groups of beneficiaries
3. Identifying and disseminating practical methods for specifying the types of benefits that would be likely to alleviate poverty among target groups

4. Developing guidelines to help mission personnel identify and use distribution mechanisms for channelling benefits to target groups
5. Developing guidelines to help AID staff identify and choose appropriate institutional arrangements for distributing benefits to selected target groups during project implementation
6. Assembling and disseminating information about monitoring and evaluation procedures that would help AID to determine the impacts of projects on beneficiaries
7. Identifying, testing, and disseminating information about the best means of distributing benefits during project implementation
8. Identifying and disseminating information about processes through which the distribution of benefits would continue or decline following the completion of development projects, and about ways in which AID can help ensure continued benefit distribution after projects are completed

The report suggested that significant improvements in designing and managing AID projects could be achieved through applied research and information dissemination, without introducing costly new management procedures.

Adapting Project Management to Local Conditions

Throughout the late 1970s, AID had been funding research on applied methods of project planning and implementation through a contract with PASITAM—the Program of Advanced Studies in Institution Building and Technical Assistance Methodology—at Indiana University. PASITAM staff did applied research and disseminated information on alternative administrative arrangements for program implementation, the effects of training on work behavior, management information systems for rural development projects, technology transfer, the effects of uncertainty on decision making, and agricultural management information systems. A number of case studies were written to illustrate the effective use of management techniques in development projects, and design notes were published to help practitioners to apply them.

In a study for the AID-sponsored PASITAM project, Stout (1980) again questioned the efficacy of the control-oriented project planning and management procedures used by the agency and prescribed for developing countries. Stout made a strong distinction between "management" and "control." Control, he argued, involves the use of methods and techniques within organizations to structure events or outcomes and to ensure that activities are in conformance with predetermined plans and decisions. Management, on the other hand, is the mobilization of knowledge and resources to cope with uncertain and dynamically complex problems, the consequences of which cannot easily be predetermined. He contended that although all organizations have a need for both management and control, the essential role of managers is to judge when each is appropriate and to maintain the proper balance between them.

A good deal of evidence from AID's own project evaluations suggested that most of the problems with which the agency and governments in developing countries dealt were complex, risky, and uncertain. They were rarely amenable to control through more rigorous or detailed management systems. Stout (1980: 6) claimed that "there is an inverse relationship between the ability to control and the necessity to manage. A controlled situation is a closed set: there are well-defined objectives and the means to realize them. But management is needed in an unregulated task environment that is risk-bearing and problematical. Managers must seek solutions to problems that threaten organizational capacity. Management is an experimental process. . . ."

Stout (1980: 151) provided some guidelines for distinguishing between situations in which control and management were most appropriate. He suggested that tasks be divided into those that were primarily concerned with *development*—that were ill-structured, risky, uncertain, and in which knowledge was limited—and that must be managed in a flexible, experimental, and adaptive way; and those that were primarily concerned with *production*—that were routine, well-structured, in which there was a high degree of consensus on values and goals, and in which knowledge was well developed—and that could be dealt with through more effective controls. Applying the wrong management approach not only increased ineffectiveness and inefficiency, he argued, but could lead to adverse consequences for both the organizations implementing AID projects and those people who were affected by their decisions and actions.

Perhaps the most widely noted result of the PASITAM work was the publication of Jon Moris's *Managing Induced Rural Development* (1981). In that study, he integrated many of the findings of the PASITAM studies with those of other researchers on project and program management to derive lessons useful to AID and other international agencies on planning and managing rural development projects.

Moris suggested again that many of the features of AID's project cycle were too complex and rigid to be applied effectively in rural areas of developing countries. The local environments in which AID projects had to be designed and implemented were far different from those assumed in AID's procedures. He noted that administrative structures in developing countries have characteristics that can create serious problems for project planners and managers. The control chain from the field to the ultimate sources of finance and support tends to be long, and in that chain decisions are frequently altered or rejected for no apparent reason. Commitments to projects and programs by officials in developing countries are often conditional and quickly modified for political reasons, and the the timing of events is frequently not subject to planned control. Thus, no matter how detailed the programming and scheduling, postponements and delays must be expected.

Moris also argued that the field units usually responsible for implementing projects are contained within extremely hierarchical administrative structures, and decisions affecting development activities are usually made or must be approved at the top. In many developing countries, however, there are strong differences in perspectives and interests between national and local administrators, and local staff are often cut off from or in conflict with officials at the center. Finally, Moris (1981) pointed out that supporting services from the central government are usually unreliable and staff at any level of administration cannot be dismissed except for the most flagrant offenses. Thus many development projects are only halfheartedly supported from the center and poorly managed at the local level.

Within this kind of administrative environment, Moris insisted, AID's design and implementation requirements were often unrealistic or perverse. To be effective, he noted, project planning and management must be a "grounded" activity in which field conditions are well understood and planners and managers are heavily engaged in day-to-day operations.

Moris pointed out that the following factors must be seriously considered in designing development projects that introduce new methods and technologies aimed at helping poor farmers. The projects must (1) offer low risks for participants; (2) provide visible and substantial benefits at the farm level; (3) offer participants regular access to cash incomes; (4) assist peasant farmers with meeting recurrent costs after the innovation is introduced; (5) avoid expanding welfare services before there is a production base that can yield revenue to pay for them; (6) use innovations that are not dependent for their adoption on loan financing in the initial phases; (7) consider long-term effects of technology transfer because these may be quite different from the immediate effects; (8) be implemented in a way that does not bypass local officials, who will remain long after outside experts and technicians have left; and (9) build administrative capacity on small and incremental, rather than on large-scale and complex, activities.

Finally, Moris (1981: 124-125) derived a number of lessons from the applied research and cases on how to manage rural development projects more effectively. Among them were the following:

1. Find the right people to lead a project and let them finalize its design if you want commitment and success.
2. Keep supervision simple and the chain of command short.
3. Build your project or program into the local administrative structure, even though this will seem initially to cause frictions and delay.
4. If the program aims at achieving major impact, secure funding and commitment for a ten-to-fifteen-year period.
5. Put the project under the control of a single agency and see that the agency can supply the necessary external inputs.
6. Attempt major projects only when the nation's top leadership is ready for change and willing to support the program.
7. Make choices about projects and contractors based on records of past performance.
8. Treat political constraints as real if you wish to survive.
9. Recruit core staff from those who have already done at least one tour of duty in an area [where the project is to be located].
10. Concentrate efforts on only one or two innovations at a time.
11. Make sure that contact staff in touch with farmers is adequately trained, supervised, motivated, and supported.
12. Identify and use the folk management strategies which managers rely upon within the local system to get things done.
13. Simplify scientific solutions to problems into decision rules that can be applied routinely without special expertise.
14. Look for the larger effects of an item of technology on the entire system before deciding upon its adoption.
15. Insure that experienced leaders have subordinates who do stand in for them on occasion and that there is a pool from which future leaders can be drawn.

Moris concluded that, realistically, development projects and programs could not be designed comprehensively and in detail—that is, in the conventional "blueprint" fashion. Many of the lessons of past experience could provide guidelines for those engaged in project planning and management, but the real challenge to both AID and governments in developing countries was to create a process of project management based on continuous learning.

5

Development Management as a Learning Process

In the early 1980s, AID's applied research and technical assistance were strongly influenced by the economic philosophy and foreign policy priorities of the Reagan administration and by the emphasis on "performance management" that had emerged from work on improving development administration that AID commissioned during the late 1970s.

In October 1981, Ronald Reagan made a foreign policy speech in Philadelphia in which he outlined his administration's guidelines for foreign assistance. Reagan called for a reexamination of assistance efforts to assure that they were not merely reinforcing the growth of the public sector, but were actively promoting private enterprise. He described five major principles that would guide his administration's international development programs. They included, first, stimulating international trade by opening up markets within and among countries; second, tailoring development strategies to the specific needs and potential of individual countries and regions; third, guiding assistance toward the development of self-sustaining productive capacities, particularly in food and energy; fourth, improving the climate for private investment and the transfer of technology accompanying such investment; and fifth, creating a political atmosphere in which practical solutions could be applied rather than "relying on misguided policies that restrain and interfere with the international marketplace or foster inflation" (USAID, 1982). The speech followed quite closely memoranda on foreign aid prepared for Reagan during the 1980 presidential election by M. Peter McPherson, a campaign advisor.

In 1981, Reagan appointed McPherson to be AID administrator. Shortly after taking office, McPherson directed the agency to pursue four high-priority objectives: the promotion of "policy reform" in national economic and political strategies of governments in developing countries, the promotion of private enterprise, transfer of U.S. technology and skills to developing countries, and institutional development. Noting that progress toward development depends in large part on government policies that either hinder or facilitate program and project implementation, McPherson encouraged USAID missions to engage in "policy dialogues" with governments to influence or persuade them to adopt and carry out policies that would promote production and distribute more widely the benefits of economic growth.

One of AID's major objectives also was to foster open markets in developing countries and to build the capacity of the private sector to participate in development activities. AID would also focus its efforts on identifying and transferring to developing countries appropriate technologies that would increase production and provide the physical and social services required to satisfy basic needs. Finally, AID would continue to strengthen the capacities of indigenous institutions in developing countries to provide essential goods and services, and would offer training to upgrade the technical skills and managerial ability of personnel within those institutions (USAID, 1983).

Not surprisingly, AID's *Development Administration Strategy Paper,* issued in 1981, closely reflected the administrator's four policy priorities. It declared (USAID, 1982: 2-3) that AID's development administration strategy included the following:

1. *Sector-specific institutional development*—improving institutional performance in policy formulation, technology transfer and program management and strengthening the capacity of institutions in high-priority sectors to provide public services and promote private investment in order to achieve "sustainable benefits for broad groups of people"

2. *Strengthening local initiative*—improving the managerial performance of local enterprises in developing countries and assisting governments to strengthen local entrepreneurship, group cooperation, local government and provincial development "in ways that stimulate local initiative and self-help, but avoid imposing burdens on the poor"

3. *Improving capacity in management service institutions*—strengthening the capacities of selected institutions in developing countries to provide relevant and practical management training, education, consulting, and applied research

4. *Policy reform*—supporting selectively reforms of economic, financial, and administrative policies and government structures through technical assistance and the application of new management technologies

The strategy placed strong emphasis on improving managerial performance in existing institutions in developing countries, and on expanding administrative capacity at levels other than the central government. It declared that

> Limited administrative and institutional capabilities remain one of the central roadblocks to effective and equitable development. The need cannot be simply defined in terms of creating new and enlarged bureaucratic structures. One of the central problems is the rate at which the size and scope of bureaucratic activity have increased. Managerial skills and effective administration are not a function of size. Furthermore, the process has tended to shift an increasing burden of responsibility for addressing socioeconomic needs from individual communities and groups to a poorly equipped central administration. As a result, many developing countries are struggling to support cumbersome, centralized public bureaucracies that are unable to carry out service delivery and investment programs at acceptable levels of effectiveness. (USAID, 1982: 8)

The strategy paper claimed to reflect many of the lessons learned through AID's experience with development administration since the early 1960s. Among the principles that were to guide the agency's technical assistance in development management during the 1980s were the following:

1. A greater reliance on *specific, incremental improvements in actual program performance* as a supplement to, or instead of, reforms of national administrative structures
2. A stronger focus on *building administrative capacity and effective managerial performance at the middle and lower levels of government* in developing countries instead of simply providing assistance for development management to the central government and expecting improvements to "trickle down"
3. Less emphasis to be given to central coordination of government services in rural areas and more to ways of *building decentralized organizational systems capable of delivering services locally,* with AID providing help in strengthening market incentives for service provision, and developing local government capability to coordinate central services in ways that respond more effectively to local needs

4. Greater attention to be given to *increasing the capacity of voluntary and non-governmental organizations to provide services* and to assume a larger number of development functions rather than relying on overburdened and weak public institutions
5. More emphasis to be given to *linking management training to job performance requirements in specific institutions* in developing countries and to linking management training with other forms of intervention to change organizational systems and incentives instead of relying on general management training as a sole solution to management problems
6. Greater attention to be given to *using Third World management institutes for job training, consulting, research, and technical assistance* in their own countries

The strategy paper pointed out the need to mobilize support from within organizations in order to enhance their effectiveness. Creating new organizations as a way of avoiding the obstacles of bureaucratic inefficiency in existing institutions would not lead to better managerial performance in developing countries. "Successful institutional change results from engaging the organization more directly with the people it serves and establishing a 'learning process' to design and implement programs that identify and address their needs," it declared (USAID, 1982: 8). "Innovations and improvements in field operations then provide the impetus for redesigning organizational structures and procedures."

The strategy paper noted that AID had been trying since 1973 to promote decentralized public service delivery and investment that would more directly benefit the poor. The results of its studies and experience with those activities emphasized the value of local participation, the need for decentralized resource mobilization and management, the need for lower-cost service delivery arrangements, the value of linkages between local and central governments and the difficulty of achieving complex, multiple objectives in resource-poor countries. "The lessons of this experience should not be lost," the strategy paper declared. "Decentralized public services and investment must continue but they must be directed to middle- and lower-level institutional and management capabilities, in ways that foster production and self-help."

Within these guidelines, the strategy paper emphasized that AID's development assistance programs must remain sensitive to the issue of equity, both in terms of who is served by development institutions and who works in them.

Managing Decentralization

In the late 1970s and early 1980s, AID began extensive research on ways of promoting administrative decentralization in developing countries. In 1979, the agency initiated a project on managing decentralization. The project proposal argued that the topic was of crucial importance to AID's development administration efforts because "decentralization is necessary to increase the scope of decisions, and thus incentives, available to local participants, as well as to build institutions and to encourage, structure, focus and stabilize such participation" (USAID, 1979: 25).

Research on decentralization was undertaken through cooperative agreements on regional planning and area development with the University of Wisconsin at Madison and on administrative decentralization for rural development with the University of California at Berkeley.

In the work done through the University of Wisconsin, Rondinelli (1980) began to develop a framework for defining decentralization and assessing the conditions necessary for promoting it. Rondinelli's review of the literature (1981: 137) and experience with decentralization in developing countries yielded a more precise definition than had been used previously in AID projects. He defined decentralization as "the transfer or delegation of legal and political authority to plan, make decisions and manage public functions from the central government and its agencies to field organizations of those agencies, subordinate units of government, semi-autonomous public corporations, areawide or regional development authorities, functional authorities, autonomous local governments or nongovernmental organizations." He argued that the degree of political or legal power that is transferred or delegated with the authority to plan, decide, or manage—that is, the amount of power that the central government "gives up" to subordinate or semiautonomous institutions—depends on the form of decentralization that is used and the amount of support that the central government provides to other organizations in carrying out decentralized functions.

The research identified four major types of decentralization that were being tried—usually with support from AID or other international assistance organizatons—in developing countries. The approach that was used most frequently in developing countries was *deconcentration,* or the handing over of some administrative authority or responsibility to lower levels within the central government—that is, a shifting of workload from centrally located officials to staff or offices outside of the national capital. This was usually done by creating field offices of national ministries at the state, provincial, or district level. A second, more extensive form of decentralization, but one used less frequently, was *delegation*. This involved the transfer of managerial responsibility for specific functions from the central government to organizations outside the regular bureaucratic structure: usually to public corporations, regional development agencies, special function authorities, semiautonomous project implementation units, and a variety of parastatal organizations. Although authority to manage specific functions was usually transferred by delegation, the central government maintained ultimate responsibility for those functions. A third form of decentralization involved *devolution*—the creation or strengthening of autonomous subnational units of government or the transfer to them of functions that were implemented outside of the direct control of the central government (the creation or strengthening of local governments was even a rarer form of decentralization). Finally, decentralization could involve *privatization,* in which governments divested themselves of some or all responsibility for functions either by transferring them to nongovernment organizations or by allowing them to be performed by private enterprises.

Reviewing the experience with decentralization in about twenty-five countries, Rondinelli (1981) found that it was encouraged by international assistance agencies and some leaders in developing countries for a variety of reasons, not all of which were necessarily consistent with each other. Decentralization was seen by some proponents as a means of overcoming the severe limitations of centrally controlled national planning that had become evident in most developing countries over the previous two decades. It was also advanced as a means of cutting through the enormous amount of red tape and the complex and rigid administrative procedures that were characteristic of decision making and management in most developing countries. Advocates of decentralization believed that by devolving functions to local governments or reassigning central government officials to local levels, government officials' knowledge of and sensitivity to local problems and needs would be increased. Some national leaders who promoted decentralization also thought that it would allow greater political and administrative "penetration" of national government policies into areas remote from the national capital and where political support was weak. In countries beset with political fragmentation, decentralization would allow greater representation for various political, religious, ethnic, or tribal groups in development decision making and thereby increase their "stake" in maintaining political stability.

Other advocates of decentralization thought that it would lead to the development of greater administrative capability among local governments and private institutions throughout a country. This would increase their ability to generate development without central government funding. Still others pointed out that decentralization could lead to greater efficiency in the central government by relieving top-level managers of having to perform routine tasks, which caused delays and bottlenecks in the decision-making process. Decentralization, some proponents contended, would also facilitate greater participation in development planning and administration.

After examining in detail the experience with decentralization in three East African countries—Sudan, Kenya, and Tanzania—Rondinelli (1981) concluded, however, that few of these alleged benefits of decentralization were being realized. More often, decentralization led to a redistribution of power and responsibility within the central government and had been undertaken primarily for political reasons. The transfer of power to the local level or to nongovernmental organizations was usually negligible. In most countries, even when formal responsibilities were transferred, central governments failed to decentralize financial resources or provide the authority to raise revenues. In some cases, decentralization failed to achieve the desired effects or had adverse consequences for local administrative units and private organizations.

The studies concluded that, although decentralization could contribute to making development administration more effective and efficient and in increasing citizen participation in development planning and management, it was a complex process that had to be carried out carefully. Rondinelli (1980, 1981) was able to identify from the experience in developing countries during the 1970s four sets of conditions that contributed to the successful decentralization of development planning and management functions.

1. *Strong central government political and administrative support,* including:
   (a) Strong political commitment and support from national leaders to the transfer of planning, decision making, and managerial authority to field agencies and lower levels of administration
   (b) Acceptance by political leaders of participation in planning and management by organizations that are outside the direct control of the central government or the dominant political party
   (c) Support of and commitment to decentralization by central government administrators and a willingness and ability to provide decentralized organizations with technical and financial support

(d) The creation or strengthening of effective channels of political participation or representation for citizens that reinforce and support decentralized planning and administration and that allow citizens to express their needs and demands and to press claims for national and local development resources

2. *Effective and appropriate organization of the decentralization process,* including:
   (a) Appropriate allocation of planning and administrative functions among levels of government, with each set of functions suited to the administrative and financial capacity of the organizations to perform them effectively
   (b) Concise and definitive decentralization laws, regulations, and directives that clearly outline the relationships among different levels of government and administration, the allocation of functions among organizational units, the roles and duties of officials at each level and their limitations and contraints
   (c) Creation of flexible arrangements, based on performance criteria, for reallocating functions as the resources and capabilities of local governments change over time
   (d) Clearly defined and relatively uncomplicated planning and managment procedures for eliciting participation of local leaders and citizens, and for obtaining the cooperation or consent of beneficiaries at various stages of project implementation
   (e) Creation of communication linkages among local units of administration or government and between them and higher levels that facilitate reciprocal interaction, exchange of information, cooperative activity and conflict resolution

3. *Behavioral and psychological changes conducive to supporting decentralization,* including:
   (a) Changes in the attitudes and behavior of central and lower-level government officials away from those that are centrist, control-oriented, and paternalistic, and toward those that increase their willingness to share authority with citizens in planning and managing development activities
   (b) Creation of effective means of overcoming the resistance, or getting the cooperation, of local elites and traditional leaders in decentralized processes of planning and administration

  (c) Creation of a minimum level of trust and respect between citizens and government officials, and a mutual recognition that each is capable of performing certain functions and participating effectively in various aspects of development planning and management

  (d) Creation of strong leadership in local governments and organizations that will allow effective interaction between local and central units of government

4. *Adequate resources for local governments and private organizations to carry out decentralized functions,* including

  (a) The transfer of sufficient authority for local units of administration or government to raise, or to obtain, adequate financial resources to acquire the equipment, supplies, personnel, and facilities needed to perform their duties in a decentralized system

  (b) Provision of adequate physical infrastructure and transportation and communication linkages among local administrative units to mobilize resources and deliver public services effectively

Thus the research carried out through the University of Wisconsin project underlined the complexity of promoting decentralization effectively, and emphasized that AID should view decentralization as an instrument for attaining limited goals rather than as an end in itself.

Many of these findings were reinforced by the work on administrative decentralization carried out for AID by the University of California at Berkeley. The Berkeley researchers came to the conclusion early on that although decentralization could be an important means of improving public participation in rural development, there were many situations it which it neither increased the efficiency or raised the effectiveness of development programs. Cohen and his associates (1981) argued that decentralization is not an end-state, because no government is completely decentralized, but a process that can be pursued in many ways. In examining arrangements for decentralization, Leonard (1982) found eight major types: (1) devolution, (2) functional devolution, (3) interest organizations, (4) prefectorial deconcentration, (5) ministerial deconcentration, (6) delegation to autonomous agencies, (7) philanthropy, and (8) marketization.

The appropriate arrangement for decentralizing any particular development project or program would depend, Leonard (1982) insisted on four variables: first, the program's vulnerability to inequality; second, the nature of local elites and their interests; third, the nature and variability of interests among national agencies, and finally, the relative capabilities of national and local organizations to meet the program's technical and administrative requirements.

After examining a variety of rural development programs carried out by organizations with decentralized functions, Ralston, Anderson, and Colson (1983: 113) concluded that decentralization worked best where there were strong local organizations:

> Regardless of the form selected, decentralization in systems with weakly organized local units usually leads to further penetration by the central power, which more often than not results in the extraction of what few local resources remain, including the most able of the local leaders. Despite legislation and administrative orders (as in Tanzania and New Guinea), decentralization usually favors the central government or the local elite. This has advantages in more realistic planning of programs to fit the local situation, but it is in conflict with the professed goal of improving the conditions of those living in extreme poverty, and is not likely to help the poorest 40 percent of the world's population.

Leonard (1982) emphasized that in any form of decentralization, the creation and maintenance of complex and effective linkages between the central government and local organizations were crucial for successful rural development. Decentralization does not imply that central government simply abandons functions that it transfers, the Berkeley researchers concluded. Indeed, decentralization usually required the central government to play a strong supporting role by providing financial assistance, monitoring and supervising decentralized activities, making technical and personnel assistance available, providing services that local organizations could not provide, and allowing representation for local and community groups in program planning and implementation.

Organizational Development in the Third World

By the early 1980s, AID's Office of Development Administration was attempting to carry out the agency's development administration strategy through two large contracts under its performance management project. One was with the Development Project Management Center (DPMC) of the U.S. Department of Agriculture and the other with the National Association of Schools of Public Affairs and Administration (NASPAA). The two organizations were to provide AID with experts who could respond to requests for assistance with management improvement from USAID missions and technical offices in Washington. They would also do applied research to refine their concepts and methodologies of project management, and they would disseminate the results of their applied research and technical assistance within AID and to developing countries. Both organizations had been working with the Office of Development Administration since the late 1970s on these tasks.

The Development Project Management Center provided assistance to AID primarily by adopting organizational development methods to improve project management and management training in developing countries. Both the "new directions" mandate and the recommendations of the Hall committee had led AID's Office of Development Administration to turn its attention again in the late 1970s to institution building and to improving public sector management training. Experiments with organizational development began in 1978, when the Office of Development Administration was requested by AID's Office of Health to provide support and assistance for health management improvement and especially with AID projects in the fields of primary health care, water and sanitation, disease control, and health planning.

The Office of Development Administration commissioned a study that reviewed health projects in developing countries and made an indepth assessment of health program management in Costa Rica, where a wide range of problems and deficiencies impeding successful service delivery were found. Rizzo, Davidson, and Snyder (1980) discovered serious deficiencies in organizational structure: e.g., excessive numbers of institutions attempting to provide health services with little or no cooperation among them; overly centralized control of authority, personnel, and resources with "a consequent isolation of the periphery from planning involvement and responsibility"; and fragmentation of responsibilities and lack of coordination.

In addition, they discovered weak planning, programming, budgeting, and financial controls. Health programs and projects were undermined by unrealistic plans, inadequate data collection, lack of participation by lower level officials or beneficiaries, unclear program objectives, weak relationships between health program planning and annual budgeting, poor financial planning, and the lack of cost accounting.

Moreover, the implementation of health programs and projects suffered from inadequate information, supervision, and evaluation. Health agencies lacked adequate information, or collected data that were neither timely nor related to the needs of decision makers. Supervision within central agencies was usually weak and evaluation of planning, budgeting, and programming was either lacking or inadequate for managers to correct deficiencies and improve service delivery. The health ministries had serious shortages of trained management personnel. Those that they did have tended to be inappropriately assigned or not used to full capacity. "The manpower system is further aggravated because of low salaries, low motivation for service in public health, and difficulty in attracting highly competent people to the services," Rizzo and his associates (1980: 6-7) pointed out. "There is usually a lack of career progression and of in-service training facilites to upgrade the managerial capabilities of the staff."

All of these problems were exacerbated by weak supply and transportation services and inadequate maintenance of supplies and facilities, especially in rural health units. In addition, health projects and programs were often poorly managed because of widespread resistence to change within the bureaucracies, inflexible regulations and procedures, and conflicts among professionals and nonprofessional staff in the health services. Doctors of medicine often controlled health service delivery agencies although most did not have adequate managerial training or capability to perform these roles effectively.

Many of these deficiencies in health programs and project management were identified by the officials and managers in the health agencies in developing countries. The study found that attempts to provide U.S. technical assistance often did not solve or alleviate these problems because U.S. experience with health program administration was different from that in less developed countries. Attempts simply to transfer health management techniques thus were inappropriate, and were only effective when serious efforts were made to adapt them to local conditions and needs. Few U.S. organizations had sufficient numbers of people who were experienced in developing countries, who could speak foreign languages and who could adapt health management procedures to other cultures.

Rizzo, Davidson, and Snyder suggested that the most effective means that AID could use to help improve health project and program management would be to assist in the funding and delivery of appropriate management training. But they insisted that conventional approaches to training would not be appropriate and suggested instead the creation of training programs based on the following principles:

1. Management training must be closely linked to organizational needs in specific developing countries. This could be done by explicitly identifying the changes that needed to be made in the organization and then translating these changes

into performance criteria for specific jobs. Changes then could be made through new knowledge, skills, and attitudes.

2. Training objectives should be determined by the types of performance required to bring about changes in the organization. Therefore it would be necessary, before training programs were designed, to distinguish between performance changes that could be achieved through training and those that required changes in policies, procedures, and incentives.

3. Training should not be a one-time occurrence, but a continuing process over a long period of time to help develop, maintain, correct, and reinforce desired behavior and performance within the organization. Much of the continuing training should be on the job and accomplished through self-learning activities.

4. Instead of concentrating on individuals, training should involve a "critical mass" of people so that that new management techniques and procedures could be applied throughout the organization. The training should be group- or team-focused and involve people at various positions in the organization's hierarchy. "Thus, the selection of trainees, the content of training, the critical mass, and the utilization of the on-the-job training are all aligned for maximum pay-off to health services."

5. The contents of and participants in the training programs should be chosen by the health organization and not by the trainers or advisors, so that the needs of the organization become the focus of the training programs.

6. All training materials—texts, cases, readings—must be drawn from or adapted to the culture, the health sector, and the organization's needs. Where such materials do not exist, some investment should be made in developing them before the training program is offered.

7. The training methods should be applied and practiced. Training courses should not be merely an intellectual exercise or a transfer of knowledge. Methods should include such techniques as role playing, case analyses, programmed instruction, simulation, field work, and others that require the participants to practice what they are learning. The methods should, the authors insisted, "reflect the fact that management is a performing art and not an intellectual discipline."

8. Training programs of this kind are usually more effectively tailored to organizational needs if they are managed in house by the health agency or in collaboration with an external in-

stitution. It is much more difficult to develop an appropriate training program if it is managed exclusively by external consultants.

9. If external consultants are used, they should be able to adapt the training program to local needs and to the culture in which it will be offered.

10. The training program should also include or make provision for research and development to adapt knowledge to local conditions, consultation and experimentation to test new methods and techniques under local conditions, and means of disseminating the results.

In the late 1970s and early 1980s, the Development Project Management Center (DPMC) devoted much of its attention to developing interventions for improving project and program management performance along the lines suggested in the health management study. The staff of DPMC relied heavily on the use of "process intervention" strategies and behavioral change methodologies, based in part on the "organizational development," or OD, approach to management improvement. Organizational development is defined in the management literature as "a process which attempts to increase organizational effectiveness by integrating individual desires for growth and development with organizational goals. Typically, this process is a planned change effort which involves the total system over a period of time, and these change efforts are related to the organization's mission" (Burke and Schmidt, 1971).

Usually, OD theorists use various forms of intervention to change group attitudes and values, modify individual behavior, and induce internal changes in structure and policy (Golembiewski, 1969). Among the methods used are (1) *process analysis* activities that attempt to increase understanding about complex and dynamic situations within organizations; (2) *skill-building* activities that promote behavior consistent with organizational development principles; (3) *diagnostic* activities that help members prescribe and carry out changes within the organization; (4) *coaching* or *counseling* activities that attempt to reduce or resolve conflicts within the organization; (5) *team-building* activities that seek to increase the effectiveness of task groups within the organization; (6) *intergroup* activities that create or strengthen linkages among task groups within the organization; (7) *technostructural* activities that seek to build "need-satisfying" roles, jobs, and structures; and (8) *system-building* or *system-renewing* activities that seek to promote comprehensive changes in an organization's larger "climate and values" (Golembiewski, Proehl, and Sink, 1981).

The process of organizational development is usually initiated and guided by external "facilitators" who induce members of the organization to identify organizational or managerial problems, to analyze the problems and the forces within and outside of the organization that inhibit or promote change, and identify alternative managerial strategies, methods, and techniques for overcoming problems. The facilitators help the organization's members to identify and diagnose the factors limiting change, select the most appropriate strategies for improving organizational and managerial effectiveness, and then to develop processes for implementing the strategy (Gibson, Ivancevich, and Donnelly, 1973). Heavy reliance is placed on job-related training in which groups from various levels in the organizational hierarchy participate in tasks designed to bring about behavioral changes.

The DPMC approach to improving management performance, however, attempted to improve upon and go beyond conventional OD approaches. It rejected the notion that there are generic management techniques that could be used by all organizations in developing countries to improve the implementation of projects and programs. But it did accept the idea that almost all organizations have common or generic functions. It asserted that improvements in management performance could be brought about by identifying common management functions and establishing processes through which appropriate management techniques could be applied to improve an organization's ability to achieve its goals.

The generic management functions identified by the DPMC staff included having (1) clearly stated and shared objectives, (2) a consensus on the strategies and means for carrying out objectives, (3) a consensus on roles and responsibilities, (4) realistic implementation planning and support systems, and (5) operational guidance and adaptive mechanisms for policy and program modification and redesign. The DPMC approach used a process of intervention that would lead the staff to identify appropriate management technologies and apply them to the generic management functions in order to improve organizational performance.

In a background study for AID's *Strategy Paper for Management Development,* Ingle and Rizzo (1981: 2) defined the "performance improvement approach" as a "process whereby people in an organized activity seek to increase its effectiveness and efficiency." Among the means to attaining higher levels of efficiency and effectiveness they prescribed training and organizational changes focused on goal setting, planning, problem analysis, feasibility analysis, and decision criteria; and on organizing activity networks, scheduling, budgeting, monitoring, and evaluation. Other tools frequently used in organizational development were also recommended, including management team building, communication, conflict resolution, and group decision making. The methods were to be instrumental in stimulating creativity, leadership, cooperation, participation, trust, willingness to experiment, self-confidence and self-reliance. They were to be applied through learning by doing, teaching by demonstration, transferring skills and values along with knowledge, coaching, group experiential learning, job enlargement, and incentives.

The basic concepts underlying this "performance improvement approach" or performance management process, as it was alternatively called, included

1. Intervening at multiple levels in an organization and training top executives, middle-level managers, and project staff in order to develop a shared commitment throughout the organization to management improvement
2. Promoting self-initiated changes within existing organizations instead of trying to change organizational structures through external forces
3. Attempting to encourage groups or teams within the organization to define and bring about needed changes in administrative behavior rather than trying to change individual behavior independently of the social processes operating within the organization
4. Emphasizing the importance of the process, as well as of outputs, through which managerial changes are made in the organization
5. Developing individual capacities through "action training," that is, by having participants apply newly learned skills and problem-solving methods to tasks that are actually related to their jobs
6. Training teams within an organization through a structured and accelerated process of learning in which they must identify organizational objectives and managerial problems and apply management techniques to increase organizational efficiency and effectiveness (Ingle and Rizzo, 1981; Solomon, Kettering, Countryman and Ingle, 1981)

Much of DPMC's work also went into the training of trainers and consultants in the processes of performance improvement and in methods of action training. DPMC staff and consultants participated in more than fifty short-term assistance projects and four long-term projects by 1982. The long-term projects included helping the government of Jamaica improve its systems of project design and implementation, providing assistance with improving financial management systems in the African Sahel, assisting with Portugal's program for agricultural production, and helping the government of Thailand design a project management information system.

In the program in the Sahel, DPMC staff developed a set of operational requirements for selecting and training trainers and consultants in its "action-training" methodology. The requirements included (Solomon, 1983): (1) an ability to initiate a training event by establishing and maintaining a supportive learning climate in which participants are willing to take risk and demonstrate new skills; (2) the ability to lead a discussion that draws lessons from the training activities; (3) the ability to manage difficult cross-cultural situations with sensitivity and tact while still accomplishing the goals of the assignment; (4) the ability to write training plans that have clear behavioral objectives and specific methodologies for reaching those objectives; (5) the ability to respond in ways that keep teams focused on their tasks and that will allow them to work together effectively; (6) the ability to present training materials in the local language; (7) the ability to give clear instructions to small task groups during simulated training exercises; and (8) the ability to express appropriate attitudes toward the efficacy of training and organizational development in promoting economic and social change.

The action-training approach was used extensively by DPMC staff in a four-year project in Jamaica to create a Jamaican team of trainer-consultants in the ministry of finance. Kettering (1980) drew from his experience in running the training programs for project management (in Jamaica) general lessons about the conditions that contributed to the success of the process intervention approach. He argued that the method was successfully applied when pressure for and commitment to change was present at various levels within the organization and when openness and flexibility within the organization was encouraged. In order to work well, a process of learning through follow-up and review had to become part of the organization's regular procedures; resources had to be available to support this approach to change; and there had to be benefits for those whose behavior was expected to change, as well as for those who committed resources to the project. The approach worked well when job security and continuity was assured for organizational staff and meaningful participation in organizational decision making was developed. Finally, in order for the process intervention approach to work effectively, at least a minimum level of consensus on means and goals had to exist already or had to evolve during the intervention.

AID's internal evaluation of DPMC's activities in performance improvement suggested that, although the individual assistance activities were generally well regarded by the organizations to which help was provided, the Development Project Management Center itself needed a more effective long-range plan for its work so that its activities added up to more than a series of unrelated interventions in developing countries. Moreover, AID noted that the processes used by DPMC had been applied in very different situations and that it was not yet a proven procedure for bringing about organizational change. Therefore, DPMC would have to analyze its own experiences more systematically to learn what actual impacts the interventions were having on organizations in developing countries (USAID, 1982a).

A Learning Process Approach to Development Management

The other major means by which AID's Office of Development Administration began to carry out the agency's development management strategy was through a contract with National Association of Schools of Public Affairs and Administration. During the late 1970s and early 1980s, NASPAA provided short-term consultants from schools of public administration in universities throughout the United States for assignments in developing countries in Africa and Central America. NASPAA consultants also assessed training programs and the management capacity of organizations in Sri Lanka, Pakistan, Tunisia, and Haiti (USAID, 1982a).

Although NASPAA pursued applied research into a number of topics, perhaps its most widely known work was that on the management of social development programs carried out by David Korten, a NASPAA field staff member assigned first to the USAID mission in the Philippines and later to the mission in Indonesia.

Much of Korten's work proved to be critical of AID's procedures for planning, designing, and managing projects aimed at promoting social change and meeting the needs of the poor. The basic tenet of Korten's argument was that the attempts by AID, other international assistance agencies, and most governments in developing countries to design projects and programs in detail in advance of implementation, using standardized and inflexible procedures (the "blueprint" approach), were ineffective in helping the poor. The project cycles used by international agencies were examples of preplanned interventions that did not allow designers and implementers to analyze or understand the needs of beneficiaries, or to allow beneficiaries to participate actively in the design and implementation of the projects. Thus the projects and programs usually ended up being ill-suited to the needs of the poor. AID could not build capacity for sustained action using the "blueprint approach"; and, even when projects were temporarily beneficial, the impacts rarely lasted long after the projects were completed. Indeed, Korten (1980) challenged the value of projects themselves, as temporary activities, in creating the kind of learning environment and flexible action needed to match the appropriate resources to the needs of poor communities, and in building the long-term cooperative arrangements through which people could solve their own problems.

Korten's approach to development management was based in part on the principles of community development, in part on theories of social learning, and in part on field assessments of successful local programs that were planned and managed in ways far different from AID's usual projects. However, Korten took the concepts beyond those underlying conventional community development in recognizing the weaknesses in "top-down" centralized planning, the need for bureaucracies to be more responsive, and the necessity of planning and managing development activities through a process of social interaction, experimentation, learning, and adjustment. Moreover, Korten focused on the need to develop "institutional capacities" to manage and learn at the same time. He saw projects as obstacles to learning because of their time-bound characteristics, and emphasized the need to develop sustained capacity within organizations to engage in development activities over a long period of time. This, he argued, would require "bureaucratic reorientation."

At the heart of Korten's (1980: 497) work was the concept of the *learning process,* in which programs are not planned in detail at the outset, but only the strategy for mobilizing, using, and sustaining local organizational capacity to solve problems is preplanned. His work with the National Irrigation Administration in the Philippines and his study of similar "people-centered" projects in Sri Lanka, Bangladesh, Thailand, and India led him to conclude that they were successful because they "were not designed and implemented— rather they emerged out of a learning process in which villagers and program personnel shared their knowledge and resources to create a program which achieved a fit between needs and capacities of the beneficiaries and those of outsiders who were providing assistance." Korten insisted that "leadership and team work, rather than blueprints, were the key elements. Often the individuals who emerged as central figures were involved in the initial stage in this village experience, learning at first hand the nature of the beneficiary needs and what was required to address them effectively."

It was exactly this learning process that was lacking in the project and program management procedures of most governments and international agencies, Korten argued, and for this reason they rarely fitted the needs and desires of the intended beneficiaries. Where the poor did benefit from such activities, they tended to become more dependent on the donors rather than developing their own capacity to solve their problems through independent action.

Korten asserted that only a development program's goals and objectives should be centrally determined by those organizations providing technical or financial resources. Operational planning and management should be left to the beneficiaries and the field representatives (change agents) who worked in the places where the activities would be carried out.

An essential part of the learning process for managing social development, Korten contended (1983: 14), is *coalition building*. Change can be stimulated and sustained only when a coalition—which cuts across formal lines of organizational authority and is composed of individuals and groups who are directly affected by the project or program, or who have the resources to plan and implement it—can be formed to take responsibility for initiating and guiding action in innovative ways. Korten argued that

> the formation of such a coalition is to the learning process approach what the preparation of a project paper is to the blueprint approach. In the latter a formal piece of paper drives the project process and encapsulates the critical project concepts. In the former these same functions are performed by a loosely defined social network. . . . In blueprint projects the project plan is central and the coalition is incidental. Planning efforts are focused on plan preparation, and implementation on its realization. By contrast, in a learning process the energies of the project facilitators are directed to the formation and maintenance of this coalition, while project documentation is a relatively incidental formality, a legitimating by-product of the coalition-formation process.

The result of coalition building is *empowerment*, the enabling process that allows the intended beneficiaries of development programs and projects to exert a more positive influence on activities that will influence the direction of their lives.

Korten (1981) explained that such a learning-process approach to program and project management would contain three basic elements: (1) learning to be *effective* in assisting intended beneficiaries to improve their living conditions or to attain other development goals; (2) learning to be *efficient* in eliminating ineffective, unnecessary, overly costly or adverse activities, and in identifying methods that might be appropriate for larger-scale applications; and (3) learning to *expand* the applications of effective methods by creating appropriate and responsive organizations to carry out development tasks.

In order to adopt a learning-process approach, Korten and Uphoff (1981: 6) argued, government agencies and international assistance organizations would have to undergo *bureaucratic reorientation.* This would require changes in bureaucratic structure to allow organizations to manage development programs through social learning and to increase their capacity for people-centered planning and innovation. This would mean more than changing individual attitudes and behavior: "The more important part involves changes in job definitions, performance criteria, career incentives, bureaucratic procedures, organizational responsibilities and the like." They argued that, just as governments must use a more participatory style of interaction with their clients, they would have to adopt a participatory process for achieving bureaucratic change.

More specifically, the elements of bureaucratic reorientation would include:

1. *Strategic management* through which an organization's leaders view its role from a strategic perspective, always reassessing the organization's objectives in terms of the degree to which it is meeting its responsibilities for maintaining human well-being and initiating new learning processes to bring about bureaucratic reorientation and organizational change

2. *Responsive reward structure* in which incentives such as salary increments, preference for posting, promotion, and the assignment of new responsibilities are provided on the basis of effectiveness in serving beneficiaries in ways that strengthen their capacity for self-help

3. *Flexible and simplified planning systems* that are attuned to the needs of beneficiaries, facilitate their participation, and are designed to allow the evolution of appropriate small-scale projects and programs through collaboration with the beneficiaries

4. *Results-oriented monitoring and evaluation* in which procedures are designed to measure and assess the degree to which benefits reach, and are effectively used by, beneficiary groups rather than the funds expended or activities completed, and in which greater emphasis would be placed on continuous self-evaluation by participants rather than periodic external evaluations

5. *Revised personnel policies* that would (a) promote more stable and longer-term assignments of staff so that they could participate effectively in the learning process, (b) require them to have substantial experience in social and organizational analysis, as well as technical specialities, and (c) structure their assignments so that they have to work in multidisciplinary teams and become conversant in local dialects and languages of the peoples with whom they were working

6. *Flexible financial management procedures* that would provide fairly predictable and stable funding levels over a period of time sufficient to facilitate the learning process, and that would allow the staff to elicit matching contributions of work and resources from participating communities

7. *Differentiated structure* in which specialized units or services could be established to serve distinct client groups, and which allowed specialization for tasks that serve special or unique needs of different groups of beneficiaries

8. *Participatory training* that would teach organizing, as well as technical skills, and use participatory methods in which problem-solving and interaction abilities of the participants could be strengthened

9. *Well-defined doctrine* that would promote a widely shared understanding of the organization's mission in helping intended beneficiaries and from which the staff could clearly delineate their purposes and responsibilities in meeting organizational objectives

10. *Use of applied social science* through which the organization could improve its capacity to gather and use data crucial to increasing its effectiveness in identifying and meeting the needs of its beneficiaries

Korten (1982) cited the Community Irrigation Committee (CIC), which was set up through the National Irrigation Administration in the Philippines, as an example of how working groups could be used as a mechanism for managing bureaucratic reorientation. The CIC evolved from a set of informal working relationships between the NIA and the staff of other agencies and organizations involved in irrigation projects; membership was informal and voluntary. The CIC served as a coalition of committed individuals in which members assumed multiple leadership roles. It had access to financial resources that could be used flexibly, and it focused its attention on overcoming bureaucratic obstacles to effective field action. Effective action would bring benefits to local communities, stimulate innovations in service delivery, provide special training and technical assistance, promote policy changes, and allow innovations to be tested in pilot projects. "Careful documentation of the interactions of agency personnel with farmers provided a good understanding of needs from the farmers' point of view and allowed for the identification of conflicts between farmer goals and agency policies and procedures," Korten (1982: 10) pointed out. "The goal was and is to learn from field-level action and to adjust policies and management systems to the needs so identified."

Other research sponsored by NASPAA explored issues related to the social learning approach to development management. Pyle's (1982) study of factors influencing the success of small-scale community health projects in India indicated that they worked well because they were characterized by (1) a "results" orientation in which objectives were clearly specified, the target groups were clearly identified, indicators of success were stated in terms of specific outputs, work was performed through team activity, and training was task-oriented and job-related; (2) a high degree of dedication on the part of the staff that was reinforced by personnel practices that rewarded them for actions that led to the program's objectives; (3) arrangements that held both the staff and community accountable for achieving the projects' intended results; (4) a high degree of community participation in the design and implementation of the projects; and (5) flexibility to react to and redirect the project as conditions and needs changed, and to delegate authority in ways that would allow managers to achieve objectives effectively.

Pyle contended that when these successful pilot projects were expanded or transferred to the government for replication, they often failed because the government agencies did not have these same characteristics. The civil service attempted to implement them through rigid, inflexible, and nonparticipative bureaucratic procedures.

Similarly, Gran (1983) attempted to identify the organizational arrangements and management practices that were used in relatively successful health and community development projects in eighteen countries. He assessed the cases in terms of management effectiveness, mobilization of resources and delivery of services, spread effects and equity, and capacity building. He found a number of factors that helped to explain their success; among the reccuring themes were that:

1. Committed people and their values mattered.
2. Social vision in the leadership was typical.
3. The organizations developed processes for continuous learning.
4. Organizations had respect for and learned from their clients and from their environment.

5. Decentralized structures and processes made such learning practical.
6. Organizations were relatively or completely autonomous from the larger environment.
7. The poor were involved in some sort of organization in which they felt some sense of ownership and responsibility.
8. In every case, new and more participatory local organizations were developed.
9. Flexibility of process and procedures was reported in many ways.
10. Most of the cases started quite small and built organizational capacity layer by layer or region by region.
11. Creativity in funding mechanisms to multiply actual resources was common.
12. Group effort was more efficient and effective than social service programs aimed at individual poor.

Gran suggested that if development projects and programs were to be made more effective, they would have to be organized and managed in ways that would promote these characteristics.

The conclusions of NASPAA's research generated controversy both within AID and among outside critics. AID's evaluation of NASPAA's work notes that significant progress had been made in developing the concepts and ideas associated with "people-centered" planning and management, but that "progress has been slower [in] defining a methodology, identifying management techniques, determining a strategy of bureaucratic reorientation, and developing training programs to prepare people for social development management" (USAID, 1982b: 49).

An assessment by the Harvard Institute for International Development pointed out that NASPAA's approach was based on a philosophy of development rather than on an empirical model (Cohen, Grindle, and Thomas, 1983). The theories were derived from observations of development activities in a limited number of countries and in situations where a few people who strongly believe in the philosophy worked closely with the agencies funding such activities.

Critics within AID and other international agencies, while often sympathetic to the underlying philosophy, pointed out that both organizational development and social learning approaches shifted the emphasis from the technical content of programs and projects, in which they have expertise, to a process of organizational intervention and community organizing in which most AID staff have little real capacity. Moreover, such an approach is difficult to make operational in international assistance bureaucracies because they are accountable to Congress, the chief executive, or their boards of governors, who are usually unwilling to provide funds for activities that they cannot describe or for processes that are likely to produce results that they cannot anticipate or control.

Even when the staff of international assistance agencies agreed that the ultimate results of aid should be to improve the lives of the poor, political and administrative constraints prevented them from simply turning over control of funds to those groups or to intermediaries that could not specify in advance either what would be done or what the results would be. Critics of the learning process approach argued that a bilateral aid agency such as AID could not obtain funds from Congress if it claimed only to be experimenting. Unless it can show specifically what must be done and what the impacts will be, it cannot compete effectively for budgetary resources with organizations that do claim a high degree of certainty for their projects.

Moreover, governments in developing countries are often reluctant to admit that they do not know exactly what needs to be done and that they are simply experimenting with approaches that may or may not lead to positive results. The blueprint approach may not achieve the intended results, critics of the learning process approach contended, but procedures such as AID's PBAR system present *an image* of careful analysis, design, and programming that is necessary to obtain the funds required to initiate and pursue technical solutions to development problems.

In a study for NASPAA that strongly advocated a "people-centered" learning process approach to social development management, Thomas (1983: 16-17) nevertheless noted other constraints to adopting it in developing countries. "The generation of power by communities and citizens' groups is frightening to political and administrative leaders. The idea of 'empowering' communities, regardless of the intentions or the anticipated development consequences, is received with skepticism or fear," he pointed out. Ruling elites in many developing countries simply do not have the political will to empower local communities to pursue development activities over which political leaders do not have control. Moreover, there is deeply embedded in bureaucracies in developing countries "a self-perceived and socially reinforced *need for certainty* among planners and managers. . . ." Thomas contends that "many government agents are unable to tolerate the absence of direct control, of clear measures of efficiency and of rationally planned outcomes." In addition, the people-centered approaches are difficult to teach; the pedagogical style of universities and training institutes is to transfer objective knowledge. Finally, there are cultural constraints. In many societies that are hierarchical in structure, in which there are distinct social and bureaucratic classes and strongly enforced rules of behavior and interaction, and in which participatory practices are not highly valued it is difficult to introduce people-centered management approaches.

Many of the lessons learned from applied research and technical assistance in development management were reflected in AID's 1982 *Development Administration Strategy Paper,* and in the Office of Development Administration's proposal (USAID, 1982b) for a six-year Performance Management Project, which was approved in 1983. The objective of the project was to improve the management of AID-supported development projects and programs. The DPMC and NASPAA would consolidate knowledge about alternative ways of improving project and program management performance, disseminate the information to USAID missions, and develop and test improved management technologies for "people-centered" program implementation and transformation of project and program plans into results. The two organizations would also do research on financial management in AID-assisted organizations, use of microcomputers in program planning and implementation, and integrating economic and social soundness analyses in the design of projects and programs. Finally, they were asked to seek ways of improving the intervention techniques of consultants engaged in promoting organizational change.

In early 1984, both organizations began an extensive research program. State-of-the-art studies were commissioned on appropriate approaches and techniques for improving development program management, strategies of managing organizational change, training strategies for increasing managerial effectiveness, and the roles of training institutes in developing countries in improving management performance. In addition, technical studies were commissioned on alternative approaches to implementing programs of management improvement; on ways of integrating social, economic and technical factors in program and project design; and on the role of consultants as "change agents" in developing countries. Work would continue on assessing financial management improvement experiences in the Sahel region of Africa, and on methods and techniques that have proven successful in managing "people-centered" development programs.

6

Development Management in AID Projects in Africa

Problems of managing AID-funded development projects in less developed countries, especially in Africa, became more serious during the late 1970s and early 1980s, and for this reason AID's Center for Development Information and Evaluation (CDIE) began an assessment of development management performance in 1984 (Rondinelli, 1986). CDIE's evaluations provided an empirical base for analyzing problems frequently encountered in development management, and yielded important insights into the impact of development management on the implementation of AID-funded projects in Africa. A review in this chapter of the findings of those evaluations also provide an empirical perspective on the findings of other research that AID had been funding on development administration and management during the 1970s and 1980s.

The evaluations of the Center for Development Information and Evaluation had three purposes: first, to identify the major factors that influenced the implementation of aid projects; second, to identify from the experience, with a sampling of projects, the practical lessons for development management; and third, to draw from those lessons implications for enhancing development management capacity in developing countries. The evaluations began with a reconnaisance of more than 1,000 projects undertaken by AID in African countries since the mid-1970s. A content analysis of factors affecting their implementation was done for a sample of 277, and an in-depth examination was made of six large-scale agricultural and rural development projects.

Development management was defined broadly as a process through which individuals and institutions in developing countries organized and used the resources available to them to achieve specific development objectives. Development management capacity was assessed by the effectiveness with which development projects were implemented. The content analysis of the 277 projects sought to determine the influence of four sets of factors:

1. The impact of public *policy* in developing countries on the formulation and implementation of development projects
2. The impact of the process and content of a project's design on its implementation
3. The impact of the political, economic, social, and cultural environoment, that is, of *contextual* factors, on project design and implementation
4. The impact of *organizational* and *administrative* factors on project implementation

The content analysis revealed the frequency with which these factors affected the projects and the problems that managers encountered during their planning, design, and implementation (Tuthill, 1985).

CDIE used these sets of management factors to analyze project implementation in intensive field studies of six agricultural and rural development projects in Africa. Multidisciplinary teams carried out in-depth field assessments of the following:

1. *The North Shaba Rural Development Project (PNS) in Zaire.* This $31 million project included about $19 million in AID loans and grants to the government of Zaire over a ten-year period from the mid-1970s to the mid-1980s. The project sought to increase food production in the North Shaba area (Rosenthal, Jackson, Mara, and McPherson, 1985).
2. *The Egerton College Component of the Agricultural Systems Support Project in Kenya.* The aim of this project was to upgrade the quality of faculty and physical facilities at the college to increase the supply of trained personnel able to provide agricultural extension services to small land holders. The project cost about $45 million, of which about $34 million was provided through AID grants and loans (Nicholson, Bowles, Gathinji, and Ostrom, 1985).
3. *The Bakel Small Irrigated Perimeters Project in Senegal.* From 1977 to 1985, this project sought to improve dry land agriculture in the Bakel River Basin by introducing irrigation systems and new cultivation practices in twenty-five villages (Seymour, McPherson, and Harmon, 1985).
4. *The Niamey Department Development Project (NDD) in Niger.* This $27 million project, funded in part by an $18 million grant

from AID, was designed to increase rain-fed agricultural production in the Niamey Department through improved farming techniques (Painter et al., 1985).

5. *The Agricultural Sector Analysis and Planning Project (ASAP) in Liberia.* A $3.2 million grant from AID sought to develop within the ministry of agriculture a stronger capacity to do sector analysis and planning so that the ministry could help traditional farmers to solve their production and marketing problems (Herman, Shaw, and Hannah, 1985).

6. *The Land Conservation and Range Development Project (LCRD) in Lesotho.* The goals of this $16 million project, which began in 1980 and was to run for seven years, were to stabilize erosion of agricultural and range lands in the project zone and thereby increase agricultural and livestock production (Warren, Honadle, Montsi, and Walter, 1985).

Although each project was somewhat different in its characteristics, the sample was representative of projects that AID was supporting in Africa. The cases identified and assessed the factors affecting the implementation of each of the projects and analyzed the relationships among the factors in shaping their outcomes. The case studies provided information about how the four sets of factors—policy, design, contextual, and organizational and administrative—identified as important by the content analysis of the sample of 277 projects, affected the implementation of these six African projects. They also yielded important conclusions about the nature of development management and about how governments in developing countries and international assistance agencies could improve management practices in public and private sector organizations working on development projects.

Many of the lessons confirmed what was already known about managing development projects in Africa. But, in confirming known problems, the cases provided some insight into their impact on AID projects in Africa, and highlighted the need for AID to cope more effectively with frequently recurring deficiencies. Other lessons from the cases challenged conventional wisdom.

Policy and Design Factors

The cases indicated quite strongly that the policies of national governments and international assistance agencies played an important role in identifying problems and opportunities for intervention and in shaping the design of development projects. National policies also had a direct impact on the implementation of projects in Kenya, Zaire, Senegal, Niger, and Liberia, and strong indirect effects on project implementation in Lesotho.

National policies played an important role in project design by influencing the definition of goals and purposes and the selection of inputs and outputs during the proposal stage. They reflected, and in some cases helped shape, the environment in which the projects were carried out and the amount of support host country governments gave them. For example, the Land Conservation and Range Development project in Lesotho resulted in part from, and was made possible by, changing government policy toward land use during the late 1970s. Although it took the government a long time to develop the capacity to implement these policies, primarily because of opposition from traditional tribal chiefs, the objectives of the LCRD project would have been difficult to achieve without policy changes and political commitment from the government. Similarly, the success of the project in Kenya to expand the capacity of Egerton College to produce graduates who could help increase smallholder output ultimately depended on changes in national agricultural pricing policies. No matter how successful the project was in expanding Egerton College, its graduates would have little real impact if national pricing policies remained adverse to small-scale farmers.

Furthermore, the evaluations clearly showed that projects can, in turn, have a strong influence on government policies and programs. Two of the projects—in Zaire and Senegal—influenced the ways in which government officials organized rural development programs by demonstrating the advantages of interacting more closely with beneficiaries, even though the projects themselves were not entirely successful in achieving their original goals.

Another frequent observation in the content analysis of the 277 African project evaluations, however, was that AID project designers often gave too little attention to policy implications in planning development activities. The failure of some of the project designers to understand adequately policy and contextual factors later adversely affected the management of the projects and, ultimately, the results. The content analysis showed that project designs were often overly ambitious and aimed at unrealistic targets in too short a period of time, that projects were designed too quickly or in far too much detail, and that the activities proposed often conflicted with traditional values or local conditions within the country where the project would be implemented. These design deficiencies restricted the actions of managers and organizations responsible for implementation.

The evaluators emphasized that, to the extent possible, project goals should be kept simple and discrete, as was done in Kenya and Senegal. They recommended that AID staff and consultants should attempt to design projects as an incremental series of tasks that could be accomplished within existing or easily expandable management capacity. But they found that in at least four of the projects—in Niger, Liberia, Lesotho, and Zaire—problems were complex and multi-faceted. Simple and discreet interventions could not be identified in advance, and multiple interests could not easily be accommodated. In such cases, they argued, goals must be defined broadly at the outset and refined incrementally during implementation. In such circumstances, development managers had to be skilled in coalition building, obtaining consensus from diverse interests, and providing a sense of direction for the participants and beneficiaries during implementation. The evaluations uncovered evidence that even in complex projects, however, planners must at least be clear about overall objectives if not about specific strategies, so that development managers can set general directions to be supported and followed by those responsible for carrying out the project's many components.

Another recurring theme in all six cases was that project designs must be flexible enough to allow for change and adaptation during implementation. The agricultural and rural development projects were found to require a long periods of time to achieve their objectives; flexibility to change direction as changes occur in policy, the socioeconomic environment, and government support; and a secure commitment of financial, technical, and human resources over a five-to-ten-year period.

Most of the factors affecting implementation, particularly in the more complex projects, could not be predicted accurately during the design phase, especially if there was a long gap between the time the project was designed and its implementation. Even exhaustive feasibility analysis and comprehensive planning could not anticipate changes in policy, contextual, and administrative conditions that affected the outcome of the projects. Nor could planners always accurately identify potential problems and opportunities, or predict with certainty the behavior of participants and beneficiaries. During the implementation of the Agricultural Sector Analysis and Planning project in Liberia, for example, there was a coup d'état and the priorities of the government in the agricultural sector changed rather drastically. Moreover, the minister of agriculture was replaced five times in as many years. After the coup, severe economic problems created budgetary constraints that adversely affected the implementation of the project. The evaluators concluded that designers should only provide the overall objectives for the project, and leave the choice of implementation strategies and tactics to the project's managers who, in any case, would be held accountable for the results.

The evaluators concluded that planners must tailor the project as closely as possible to local conditions and needs, even if this reduces the potential for widespread replication. They also emphasized a seemingly obvious but often neglected point: that sufficient and appropriate inputs must be provided by AID and the host country governments in order for projects to be implemented effectively, and that some discretionary funds should be provided for project managers to respond to changing needs during implementation. AID should not only provide resources that are directly related to the acheivement of a project's goals, but also those that indirectly affect implementation by establishing the project organization's legitimacy and by creating support among potential participants and beneficiaries. Projects should include resources that enable them to provide quick, visible results in order to meet the immediate needs of participants and beneficiaries, as well as inputs for achieving longer-term, more fundamental changes.

These findings implied that AID should give more careful attention in designing projects to the potential impacts of policies on project implementation and to the policy changes that may be needed in order for the project's objectives to be met. Provisions for policy changes should be made during early negotiations with host country governments, in "conditions precedent" to loans, and in performance criteria for the release of AID funds during project implementation.

Finally, the evaluations concluded that, although national policies influence the outcome of projects, AID could neither predict with certainty the impacts of policy changes nor always convince the government to make the changes necessary to implement the project effectively. In any case, policy changes alone were not sufficient to guarantee effective implementation. Successful implementation also depended on appropriate design, a conducive environment, and effective organization and administration.

Environmental and Contextual Factors

Contextual and environmental factors—the political, economic, social, and cultural conditions under which a project had to be carried out—affected implementation in more than 88 percent of the 277 African project evaluations included in the content analysis. For example, more than 17 percent of the evaluations claimed that AID's project-planning and management procedures were incompatible with or adversely affected social, cultural, or economic conditions in the host country. Nearly 26 percent indicated that environmental conditions were not conducive to implementing the projects as they were designed.

Among the lessons drawn from the six case studies were two outstanding ones. First, the social, cultural, and economic environment in a country is a major factor influencing project implementation. For example, traditional institutions and practices were seen as obstacles to implementing the project as it was designed in Zaire, Niger, Liberia, and Lesotho, but in Kenya and Senegal they were found to be useful instruments through which the staff and the local population participated in development activities. In cases where traditional institutions and practices clashed with modern management needs—as they did in Niger, Lesotho, and Liberia—project planners and managers had to make difficult choices about which of them they would attempt to change.

Second, all of the evaluations found that the degree to which host country governments supported projects also influenced their implementation. Where political support was strong, as in Kenya and Senegal, it contributed to more successful implementation. The lack of support—or, more frequently, weak support—had deleterious effects in Liberia and Zaire. When government financial support for the project was not forthcoming in Zaire, strong local leadership and effective internal management were needed to overcome the resulting problems.

The evaluations indicated that contextual factors often could not easily be changed, but that they at least had to be understood so that projects could be managed effectively within existing constraints and that appropriate strategies for coping with them could be developed.

Organizational and Administrative Factors

The evaluations identified a broad range of organizational, administrative, and procedural factors that affected the implementation of the six African development projects.

Organizational Structure

Organizational problems arose in more than 91 percent of the 277 African project evaluations subjected to content analysis. The most critical were inadequate support systems and ineffective organizational relationships.

The lessons drawn from field evaluations of the six agricultural and rural development projects were as follows:

1. The "organizational culture" in which all six of the projects were carried out shaped the opportunities for and created constraints on effective administration. The organizational culture in African countries rarely conformed to Western images of efficient and rational procedures that were often called for in the project designs, and rarely were technical advisors able to change the local culture sufficiently to enable foreign methods and techniques to work as effectively as they thought they should. Given this experience, the evaluators pointed out that an appropriate organizational structure for a project is a crucial variable in its success, but that there are no universally applicable arrangements. In some cases, strengthening existing organizations was most effective; in other cases, new organizations had to be created to overcome constraints and obstacles to change.

2. The cases shed some light on the most effective internal organizational arrangements. Although a high degree of centralization and hierarchy characterized most of the institutions that implemented the projects in these six African countries, the decentralized organizations that implemented the projects in Zaire, Senegal, and Kenya seemed to be more effective in devolving responsibility and authority. They also seemed to be more effective in strengthening administrative capacity at middle levels of management, in keeping organizations more responsive to clients and beneficiaries, and in developing a sense of "ownership" among project staff and participants. Managers in decentralized organizations could discern changes in their environment more easily, provide better feedback to top management, and elicit more effectively the participation of beneficiaries than those in centralized bureaucracies.

3. The cases emphasized that organizational changes required to achieve project goals must be deliberately planned and carried out as part of project design and implementation. Sufficient resources must also be provided for bringing about those changes. It cannot be assumed that organizational reforms will occur automatically as the result of policy changes or of

technical activities pursued during the implementation of a project. The Liberian and Zairian cases, especially, found that trade-offs had to be made in the design phase between the amount of time and resources that would be devoted to achieving technical objectives and those that would be committed to achieving organizational reforms. When strategies were not well developed for both sets of activities, the attention given to one during implementation was usually at the expense of the other.

4. One of the strongest conclusions to emerge from the cases was that sufficient flexibility must be given to development managers to make changes in organizational structures and institutional arrangements during a project's implementation; the impact of organizational structure could not be accurately predicted during the design phase and changes in leadership, resources, environment, and policies all affected the efficacy of the project implementing unit. In Zaire, for example, the ability of the managers of the North Shaba project to abandon the farmers cooperatives called for in the project design, when it became clear that farmers were opposed to them, allowed the project to proceed more effectively.

5. The case studies also came to strong conclusions about interorganizational relationships in project implementation. The creation of strong supportive linkages between organizations implementing development projects and others performing complementary tasks were found to be essential for successful implementation. However, the project organizations in Kenya and Senegal that had a high degree of autonomy and independence in decision making, and control over resources and operations, seemed to be more successful than those that were under the close control of central bureaucracies.

The cases indicated that an appropriate balance between independence and accountability must be struck in designing organizations for project implementation. Projects that were located in remote or isolated areas in Zaire, Senegal, and Lesotho required a large amount of autonomy, independence, and control over their own resources in order to respond effectively to local needs and demands. However, they also needed adequate financial, technical, and logistical support from external organizations or higher levels in the bureaucracy to operate efficiently under hardship conditions. In all of the cases, informal networks of cooperation and interaction with higher-level bureaucracies, supporting organizations, and beneficiary groups were as important—and usually more so—than formal organizational linkages.

6. Coordination among government agencies and private organizations was critical in the implementation of all of the AID-funded development projects. But the evaluators found that coordination depended more on the creation of incentives and inducements than on formal requests or orders to cooperate. Coordination and cooperation depended ultimately on the degree to which various groups and organizations identified favorably with the goals of the project, obtained benefits from it, or saw their own interests enhanced by its success. Not surprisingly, cooperation was easier to elicit in projects such as the Bakel River Basin program in Senegal, in which managers developed a sense of "ownership" among participants and beneficiaries.

Also, the case studies found that sustaining the benefits of development projects depended on building local and national institutions capable of making decisions, allocating and using resources, and managing their own development activities effectively after international funding ended. Planning for the transition from temporary project organizations to sustainable institutions was an important management task in all six cases, but government and AID officials did not give it careful attention in any of the projects except the one in Kenya.

7. The evaluations found that, while supervisory functions of the USAID missions could improve project implementation, foreign assistance personnel should not attempt to intervene too strongly in the ongoing operations of the implementing organization unless it so requests. AID's role should be to develop a sense of "ownership" and responsibility in the implementing organization, and to help provide the resources necessary for it to accomplish its tasks.

Administrative Procedures and Practices

The content analysis found that 87 percent of the 277 AID projects in Africa encountered administrative problems. The evaluations of the six agricultural and rural development projects suggested that the lack of or weaknesses in formal administrative systems obstructed the successful completion of some of the projects, but that formal management systems were not always essential preconditions for success. Appropriate informal and indigenous administative procedures worked as well, if not better, than formal systems in Kenya, Zaire, and Senegal, where projects had strong leadership and committed staff. Relatively simple, informal, indigenous procedures were usually more appropriate and effective in developing countries than complex, formal, Western systems. Administrative procedures that delegated responsibility and decentralized functions were the most direct and effective way of developing the managerial capacity of middle-level staff in project organizations.

Also, different types of administrative procedures—with different skill requirements—were often needed for different components of a project. In the projects in Zaire and Senegal, for example, it was found that the more formal administrative systems used by the project-implementing unit were usually too complex or sophisticated for beneficiary groups or small-scale organizations operating in rural areas. The evaluators concluded that administrative systems must be tailored to the needs, capabilities, and resources of the groups who will use them—again a seemingly obvious lesson that was only sporadically heeded in the African projects.

The evaluations pointed out that one implication of these findings is that the administrative procedures of AID and of governments in developing countries should provide sufficient latitude for project managers and staff to be creative, innovative, and responsive to the project's beneficiaries. Administrative procedures should balance flexibility for managers to respond to complex and uncertain conditions with accountability for achieving development goals. AID's administrative procedures should support the host country's development institutions, and not constrain them as they did in several of the African projects.

Management of Financial and Technical Resources

About 86 percent of the 277 projects included in the content analysis had deficiencies in financial and commodity management. The case studies indicated that, in those projects in which the distribution of large amounts of supplies and equipment was essential to achieving project goals, appropriate commodity procurement, storage, inventory, and distribution systems had to be established quickly if other components of the project were to be implemented effectively. But the case studies also found that an important element of effective commodity management was the procurement of equipment and supplies that were appropriate to the needs of participants and beneficiaries and to the conditions under which the project had to be carried out. This principle was not applied in the projects in Niger, Senegal, and

Kenya, where "tied aid" requirements led USAID missions to order U.S.-made equipment regardless of its appropriateness. The evaluators recommended that, in cases where "tied aid" requirements conflict with the needs of the project, AID should routinely approve procurement waivers.

In the projects that depended heavily for their success on the provision of commodities, logistics management was most effective when it was made the responsibility of a full-time experienced staff member or unit and when AID-provided adequate training and technical assistance to support the logistics managers, as was done in Zaire. Special attention had to be given to establishing a special, reliable procurement and supply network for projects located in physically remote or distant rural areas that were at the "tail end" of the government's regular supply channels.

The case studies concluded—somewhat in conflict with conventional wisdom—that although formal financial management systems could enhance the project organization's implementation capacity, the existence of elaborate procedures or Western-style practices was not usually a precondition for success. The projects in Kenya, Zaire, and Senegal were quite successful using indigenous or rudimentary procedures that were sometimes not considered adequate by AID. Indeed, severe problems arose in projects in Senegal and Niger from the attempt by AID to impose its own accounting and reporting standards.

The evaluators suggested that whenever possible AID should allow project implementing organizations to use indigenous accounting systems to obtain financial information, or assist them to adapt indigenous procedures, before insisting on the use of new or separate procedures that only produce financial reports for AID. They also recommended that aid agencies provide adequate training in financial management to allow project-implementing organizations to meet their financial reporting and accounting obligations, as well as to do long-term financial and budgetary analysis of recurrent costs. In brief, they argued that AID should not impose special requirements on development organizations without providing the resources to assist them in meeting those responsibilities.

The management of technology transfer was also important because all of the AID-funded projects in Africa had a technological component. However, other factors such as leadership, commitment, and a sense of ownership and participation by beneficiaries turned out to be as important—if not more crucial—than the kind of technology that was transferred. The cases showed that inappropriate technologies were introduced in some of the projects because of organizational inertia or the failure to assess the feasibility of technology transfer before proceeding with testing or application. Problems arose because of the unresponsiveness of some project designers and managers to the desires and needs of beneficiaries, or because political criteria took priority over local needs.

The evaluators reaffirmed a lesson learned in many other AID projects: that serious attention must be given in project design and implementation to selecting technology that is appropriate to local conditions and that is simple, low-cost, and adequate to the needs of its intended users. They argued that technologies transferred to developing countries should be within the "management capacity" of the organizations that will disseminate and use them. More sophisticated technologies should be introduced incrementally only as the need arises and as the management capacity of the implementing organization expands. And they urged AID to give more serious attention to ways of adapting indigenous technologies, or of supporting indigenous efforts to develop local technologies, before prescribing the transfer of technologies from the United States. Adequate training and support systems had to be provided for using and maintaining equipment and supplies transferred to developing countries.

Human Resource Management

The content analysis of the sample of 277 projects found that over 88 percent encountered human resource management problems. The lack of adequately skilled, competent, or experienced staff, high turnover rates among trained staff, and low levels of motivation or commitment among personnel were the most frequently cited problems. In addition, about 21 percent of the evaluations cited problems with managing the participation of beneficiaries, creating interest in the project among intended beneficiaries, and implementing management improvement programs.

First, the predominant conclusion from all six field evaluations was that strong leadership was a necessary condition for successful project management, and that other factors generally could not compensate for weak leadership. The Bakel project in Senegal, an irrigation and crop production assistance program, provided the most graphic example of the importance of administrative and political leadership. During the project's early years, the implementing organization—SAED—was in constant conflict with farmers in the Bakel river basin. Irrigation supplies were not delivered to the project—or to the farmers—on time. SAED gave farmers little or no guidance about how to construct their irrigation canals and dikes. SAED paid below-market prices for the commodities that farmers had previously contracted to sell to the project, and farmers were restricted to growing crops that SAED, but not the farmers, considered to be of high priority. Not surprisingly, many dissatisfied farmers broke their contracts with SAED and complained bitterly to local and national government officials.

After an investigation by the prefect of the Department of Bakel, the director of SAED was replaced by a manager more sensitive to the needs of farmers in the region and more willing to exert strong leadership to achieve the project's goals. Changes occurred in the project almost immediately. SAED's organizational structure was decentralized to make it more responsive to its clientele. The new director allowed farmers to choose the crops that they would grow and to sell portions of their crops on the open market. He encouraged them to experiment with new ways of cultivating and harvesting their crops. The new director traveled freqently during his first six months in office, listening to farmers' grievances and discussing their problems with them.

The change in leadership in the project produced tangible results. Rice production increased dramatically. Rapid advances were made in constructing village storehouses. Local cooperatives began managing seed and fertilizer distribution on their own. And joint decision-making committees were formed by SAED and the villagers to manage project activities and maintain equipment at the local level.

The other cases also showed that a project's legitimacy, acceptance, and support depended heavily on the motivation, commitment, and responsiveness of project leaders to the needs of beneficiaries, project staff, and personnel in other participating organizations. And the degree to which projects and programs were successful in promoting institutional development depended in large measure on whether or not project managers and staff took an active role in managing and controlling the project—as in Kenya, Zaire, and Senegal—rather than passively leaving its implementation to technical assistance advisors and the USAID mission.

Second, the evaluations confirmed that different leadership styles were appropriate to different situations and phases of a development project or program. In the Senegal project, for example, a charismatic, visible, and dynamic leader was most effective. In the Kenya project, on the other hand, a collegial, low-key, and participatory style of leadership was most appropriate. The cases concluded that adequate means must be developed to assess leadership impacts on a project during implementation, and to reorient or replace managers who are not providing appropriate leadership and direction.

Third, the cases also showed that leadership must be developed throughout a project organization and not only among top managers or administrators. The motivation, commitment, and responsiveness of staff in pursuing development goals in the six agricultural projects depended, to a large degree, on the incentives offered to them to act creatively in dealing with problems and exploiting opportunities. One implication was that leadership training should be given to managers at various levels of responsibility within implementing units. Participatory management was found to be a valuable instrument of human resource development and helped strengthen the planning, decision-making, and administrative skills of those individuals and groups that participated in the projects. Training was found to be one of the most effective means of increasing managerial capacity in project implementation and of sustaining benefits, but only if it was appropriate to local needs and requirements.

Last, the evaluations emphasized that high turnover rates among staff and leaders in all of the projects, save the one in Kenya, weakened implementation. It was an especially serious problem in Liberia and Senegal. Stability in personnel assignments among technical assistance advisors, project staff, and host country counterparts was found to be essential for effective project management. One suggestion emerging from this observation was that financial, professional, and career mobility incentives must be designed for a project to recruit and retain good staff. Innovations such as dual technical and administrative promotion and pay tracks, and the provision of special amenities such as housing and educational allowances, are often necessary to keep good technical and managerial staff in projects located in remote rural areas.

In summary, the evaluations showed that development management is more than the application of a particular set of administrative systems or of scheduling, procurement, and financial management techniques. The evaluations confirmed that development management is a *process* by which leaders organize and use effectively the resources available to achieve specific development objectives. In the African projects, it involved *good judgment* in interpreting how the variety of factors influencing the achievement of project goals should be dealt with, and how the proper organizational arrangements, administrative procedures, and management techniques could be applied in varied settings to achieve specific development objectives. The evaluations concluded that much more attention needs to be given by AID, and by governments in developing countries, to personnel selection for project management in order to ensure that managers have leadership and administrative experience, as well as technical capabilities.

The evaluations implied that lessons of experience cannot easily be reduced to simple universal rules. The cases showed clearly that development managers deal with complex problems, opportunities, and environments. Managers worked in situations and with problems that were fraught with uncertainty. Development managers had to make complex trade-offs that reflected these uncertainties (Honadle, 1985). Attempts by AID agencies to impose uniform, universal, and rigid administrative systems and procedures on project organizations in developing countries were likely to lead to more rather than fewer problems during implementation.

Finally, an important implication was that training programs to enhance development management capacity must distinguish between the human element of management—consisting of leadership, judgment, experience, and creativity—and the technical element—management systems, regulations, and techniques through which routine tasks are carried out—and which Leonard (1984) refers to as "bureaucratic hygiene." Most training programs for project planning and implementation concentrated almost entirely on the latter. Although improvements in technical aspects of implementation were necessary in AID's projects in Africa, they clearly were not sufficient. Leadership, judgment, experience, and creativity were usually the most critical variables in the successful implementation of AID-sponsored development projects, and were most often neglected in management training and improvement programs.

7

Prospects for Improving
Development Management Through
Foreign Aid Programs

This review of AID's experience in providing development administration and management assistance indicates clearly that the
agency's concepts of development administration and its approaches
to development management changed quite drastically from the late
1940s to the late 1980s. Much of the change was evolutionary. It was
based in part on changes in AID policies and priorities and in part on
the accumulation of knowledge. Evaluations found that some approaches to and methods of development management assistance
were not effective in developing countries; others seemed to contribute to greater managerial capacity and more successful projects.

It should be kept in mind that each of these approaches to development administration evolved from perceptions of the needs and conditions in developing countries at different periods of time, and were in
part the results of the successes and failures of previous attempts at
improving administrative capacity in developing countries. But each
also focused on different levels of administration, and placed a different emphasis on different administrative problems: organizational
structures, administrative processes, the management of financial
and technical resources, human resources and behavioral changes
among development administrators, or policy and environmental factors. Table 7.1 provides a profile of the major theories or approaches of
development management used in AID over the past three decades
and categorizes them by their primary form of intervention.

Table 7.1 Focus of Intervention in Development Management Assistance Efforts

Institutional and Managerial Development Approaches	Focus of Intervention				
	Organization, Structure, Institutional Change	Change in Administrative Process	Improvement of Resource Input Management	Human Resources and Behavioral Change	Change in Contextual Factors
Tool-oriented Technology Transfer		X	X		
Community Development Movement	X	X			
Political Development and Modernization	X	X			X
Institution Building	X	X			X
Project Management Systems		X	X		
Local Action and Capacity Building	X			X	X
Organizational Development	X	X		X	
Behavioral Change	X			X	
Learning Process		X		X	
Bureaucratic Reorientation	X	X		X	X

Changing Trends in Development Administration

During the 1950s, U.S. development administration assistance was focused primarily on transferring managerial techniques and organizational structures that seemed to be successful in the United States to developing countries. The aim was to create rational, politically impartial, and efficient national bureaucracies in the Weberian tradition. U.S. foreign aid was invested heavily in establishing institutes of public administration in developing countries that would teach "modern" methods of management and through which the techniques and tools of Western administration would be disseminated.

During the 1960s, the emphasis shifted from merely transferring the tools of U.S. public administration to promoting fundamental political modernization and administrative reform. Development administration was viewed as a process of social engineering in which national governments assumed the primary role of stimulating economic growth, promoting social change, and transforming traditional societies. Much of AID's assistance was focused on finding ways of overcoming obstacles and breaking bottlenecks to development, especially by improving the management of agricultural, population-planning, small-scale industrial, and community development projects, and through educational reform, land redistribution and tenure reform, and road and infrastructure construction. A great deal of attention was also given to institution building as a way of strengthening the administrative capacity of organizations in developing countries to promote and institutionalize change. AID and other assistance organizations spent large amounts of money to bring people from developing countries to the United States for professional education in schools of public administration and political science, and to strengthen the capability of foreign schools of public administration for building institutions in their own countries.

Both the "Point Four" technology transfer and the political modernization and administrative reform approaches to development administration came under increasing criticism during the late 1960s and early 1970s for being ethnocentric and for attempting to transplant Western concepts of administration that were often irrelevant or inappropriate in developing countries. The "tool-oriented" approaches had transferred techniques that merely attempted to increase efficiency in carrying out routine maintenance tasks and did little to help policy makers and administrators to cope with the complex and uncertain problems of change in their own political and cultural environments. The administrative reform and institution-building approaches were often based on abstract theories that were difficult and expensive to implement. Assessments of attempts to implement them in a number of developing countries found that they often had little impact on stimulating change or restructuring administrative practices and behavior.

During the 1970s, AID's development administration assistance was refocused on improving systems management in agriculture, health and nutrition, population planning, and education and human resources development sectors. Attention was given to modeling sectoral systems and providing technical assistance and training to improve management practices. AID's applied research, technical assistance, and training also heavily emphasized the management of projects as an integrated system or cycle of activities, and AID invested heavily in adapting project management systems used in U.S. organizations to the needs of developing countries.

With Congress's "new directions" mandate to focus U.S. foreign assistance on the needs of the poor majority in developing countries, AID's development management activities were again redirected. They sought not only to expand the capacity of organizations to manage projects and programs efficiently, but also to bring about a more equitable distribution of benefits. Greater attention was given to ways in which governments might alleviate the high levels of poverty in rural areas, elicit participation of the poor in project planning and management, and design projects to distribute benefits more effectively to "target groups." They attempted to organize projects to make them more appropriate to local conditions in developing nations so that the benefits could be sustained after projects were completed (Rondinelli, 1984).

More emphasis was placed on improving the capacity of public agencies to respond to the needs of the poor by providing basic services and facilities that would stimulate productivity and raise the incomes of disadvantaged groups and by creating conditions in which community, private, and voluntary organizations could take a stronger role in "bottom-up" processes of development planning. Means were sought to help development institutions cope more effectively with the complexity and uncertainty of development activities. The focus of training shifted from transferring "objective knowledge" to promoting action-oriented, organizationally based skill building in which on-the-job instruction, problem solving, and behavioral changes were emphasized.

During the early 1980s, AID further focused its assistance on promoting policy changes in developing countries, on transferring appropriate technology to increase productivity and raise the incomes of the poor, on promoting private enterprise as an alternative to direct government provision of goods and services, and on institutional development as a way of increasing the capacity of a wide variety of private, voluntary, and local organizations to participate in development. It sought to increase the capacity of central governments to strengthen the managerial performance of subnational institutions in program and project planning and implementation. Substantial investments were made in developing and applying process interventions for improving managerial performance and bringing about long-term organizational development. Applied research and technical assistance were also focused on ways of reorienting bureaucracies in developing countries to make them more innovative and responsive to the needs of beneficiary groups. A learning process approach emerged as a major strategy for managing social development programs and reorienting bureaucracies toward implementing "people-centered" development activities more effectively.

The Emerging Challenges in Development Management

In brief, AID has experimented with, tested, and applied a wide variety of management development theories in its technical assistance and training programs since the 1950s in search of the most effective means of strengthening institutions involved in development and of increasing the managerial capacity of people involved in implementing development projects and programs. The trend in theory over the past decade has been away from the Point Four approach used during the 1950s and 1960s, in which U.S. public administration principles and procedures were simply transferred to developing nations with little or no adaptation. It has moved much more toward an approach that examines the needs and conditions of beneficiaries of aid programs in developing countries, and tailors administrative and organizational solutions to them with their participation and collaboration. Theory has also advanced beyond attempting to bring about sweeping political and administrative reforms such as those reflected in the political modernization, community development, and institution-building movements. It now emphasizes narrower organizational interventions that can improve management and administration incrementally. The trend has also been away from attempting to expand the managerial capacity of only central government ministries and toward strengthening the managerial capabilities of local, private, and nongovernmental organizations. Finally, theory has moved from strategies that attempt strengthen centralized, control-oriented, comprehensive management systems toward those that try to create more flexible, adaptive, innovative, responsive, and collaborative methods of administration in which the intended beneficiaries of development programs can participate more effectively in planning and implementing them.

Emerging concepts of development management recognize clearly that the control-oriented systems approaches to project and program management, which may have been appropriate for capital investment and physical infrastructure construction projects, may be neither effective nor efficient in projects promoting social change and human resource development. Projects aimed at promoting social and behavioral changes require a more strategic, adaptive, experimental, and learning-based process that is responsive to people's needs and desires (Rondinelli, 1983).

However, AID continues to use control-oriented management processes that attempt to anticipate and plan for all aspects of a project's implementation prior to its approval. It continues to rely on methods and procedures of project design, selection, and implementation that assume a high degree of knowledge about what needs to be done and of certainty in a world in which "the correct solutions" are not always clear—in which the only certainty is that there will be a large degree of uncertainty surrounding the most effective way of promoting economic and social change in developing countries. It makes use of methods developed primarily for capital investment projects even though the largest portion of its investment portfolio is in human development activities in agriculture, population, and education. It still relies heavily on transferring U.S. technology to solve social development problems that are not always amenable to technological solutions.

Thus the shifts in theories of development administration away from control-oriented approaches toward adaptive learning, local action, and assisted self-help have not been clearly reflected in AID management practice. Although the theory of institutional and managerial development has advanced over the past thirty years, nearly all of the approaches described earlier are still used—and have some degree of currency—within AID.

There has always been and continues to be a wide gap between the theories about how development projects and programs should be managed—many of which evolved in part through AID-sponsored research and technical assistance experience—and the procedures that AID actually uses to design and manage the vast majority of the projects and programs that it funds.

Closing the Gap Between Knowledge and Practice

One of the important challenges facing development administration theorists and practitioners is how to close the large gap that now exists between what is known about effective development management and current practice.

The degree to which AID can refine and apply the findings of development administration studies will depend on the degree to which the philosophies underlying them can be made more widely acceptable within AID, Congress, and the executive branch. The findings clearly conclude that the primary beneficiaries of assistance projects and programs should be the people of developing countries, and that AID's own project management procedures should be aimed at creating and sustaining the capacity of people to help themselves more effectively.

However, projects and programs aimed at building local capacity for self-sustaining development often require an approach to development administration that is not easily promoted through AID's "blueprint" procedures. Moreover, AID still operates in an environment in which foreign assistance is seen primarily as an instrument of achieving the goals of U.S. foreign policy and of transferring U.S.-made goods and technical expertise. Although strong and valid arguments can be made for both perceptions of the role of foreign aid, these two philosophies are not always compatible. Differences in philosophy underlie much of the debate over control-oriented and learning process approaches to development management.

Also, the perception that AID's comparative advantage is in the transfer of U.S. technology and expertise is still strong within the agency. The belief that it is the application of new technologies that lead to major economic and social changes, and that administrative or managerial improvement is either incidental or something that will come about through technologically led development, is still pervasive in AID. In many ways, more adaptive approaches to management improvement contradict the assumption that technology transfer will always solve development problems and that U.S. experts always know what needs to be done to improve the living conditions, increase the productivity, and raise the incomes of people in developing countries. AID's project cycle and its emphasis on detailed planning and design of projects prior to their approval clearly reflect the "engineering" approach to development, which was characteristic of the physical construction projects that AID sponsored through much of its early history.

This is not to say that the concepts of foreign assistance have not changed within AID since the Point Four period. They have. Nor is it to imply that AID's procedures of project and program management are so inflexible as to prevent the introduction and testing of new ideas. As this study clearly attests, AID has been a leading sponsor of research into new ideas in development management, and has provided opportunities to test those ideas in its projects and programs. Yet there is also a wide gap between the findings about how projects and programs should be designed and managed in order to build the capacity of people in developing countries to help themselves and the procedures that AID actually uses to design and manage the vast majority of the projects that it funds.

Criticisms of AID arise primarily from the dissatisfaction of advocates of two competing concepts of effective management. There are those who believe that foreign aid administration is a bureaucratic function that must be closely supervised and controlled in order to assure efficiency and effectiveness in the use of public funds to achieve larger political ends. On the other side are those who think that foreign aid's primary purpose is to improve the living conditions of the poor in developing countries, and therefore it must be managed in a flexible, responsive, and adaptive way.

AID's attempts to balance the mandates implied by these two perceptions often leave advocates of both dissatisfied. One calls for increased controls on AID's operations by Congress and the executive branch, the other insists that bureaucratic management is inappropriate and ineffective for promoting development.

More flexible, adaptive, and responsive methods of development management have been proposed increasingly over the past decade to replace existing control-oriented management procedures, which even AID's own evaluations find deficient. Yet, after more than a decade of criticism, progress in adopting new approaches to aid administration has been slow. Although the "performance gap"—which is usually considered essential by organizational theorists for bureaucratic change—is well documented, other obstacles seem to inhibit change in the AID bureaucracy. The difficulties of reconciling two largely incompatible perceptions of good management and the problems of adaptation and change in the AID bureaucracy are numerous. The political vortex in which AID must operate often creates stronger pressures to respond to demands for control in order to satisfy executive policy and congressional audit requirements, and in turn leads to difficulties in reconciling its bureaucratic and developmental tasks. The agency often applies what Simon (1960) terms "programmed decisions" to satisfy demands for control to development situations that require nonprogrammed responses. The high priority given to controlling operations often undermines or drives out the incentives for organizational learning about effective development management.

But a good deal of evidence from evaluations of AID operations suggests that the control-oriented management systems now used in the agency do not, in fact, give AID administrators effective control over project and program implementation. Although AID often requires large amounts of information during project design and approval stages, and frequently contracts for extensive studies during implementation, relatively little of that information is actually used for decision making in project planning and approval. Nor is it widely disseminated within the agency so that the AID staff can learn from it. The U. S. General Accounting Office (1982: 15) notes that "our review of AID procedures showed that AID did not have an effective system in place for collecting and disseminating information generated in the process of its own development assistance efforts."

In addition, studies by the General Accounting Office (1982) indicate that AID's management systems have not been effective in expediting the implementation or completion of projects. Only 345 projects begun after 1973 had been completed by 1981. Although AID had about $11 billion in funds obligated for projects between 1973 and 1981, the cost of the 345 completed projects totaled less than $1 billion. Between 1975 and 1981, delays in project completion increased the number of the agency's projects in the "pipeline" by more than 300 percent. By fiscal year 1982, AID had more than $3.1 billion in development assistance and more than $3.6 billion in economic support funds in its pipeline. Moreover, the GAO auditors found that "the length of time that project funds have remained unspent has increased significantly, going from an average of 16 months in 1975 to over a 23-month average in 1981."

Even if AID's management procedures were more effective in controlling the identification, design, implementation, and completion of projects, many critics argue that the very attempt to design projects in detail prior to their activation and to control stringently their implementation are inappropriate for development activities. Such attempts often have adverse impacts on intended beneficiaries. Development, they argue, is a process in which poor people and countries learn to help themselves so that they can solve problems without depending on external aid. But AID's control-oriented management procedures have encouraged the design of projects *for* people in developing countries, and usually without the participation of intended beneficiaries. As the representative of one private voluntary organization, which has served frequently as an AID contractor, emphasized in congressional testimony: "A proposal initiated by one group in a country usually is not ready for implementation until two years later when the people involved have changed." He argued that the "strange notion that planning of people-oriented proposals should be done by someone other than the group who will carry out the program imposes rigid and artificial designs which are usually not implementable and plans have to be done over by whoever gets the contract" (Taylor, 1984: 455).

Obstacles to Change in the AID Bureaucracy

As this review of AID's experience has shown, substantial evidence has been accumulating for more than a decade that AID's control-oriented approaches to project and program administration are neither effective in controlling aid activities nor appropriate for promoting economic and social change in developing countries. Alternatives have been proposed for nearly as long. Why, then, has there been so little change in the AID bureaucracy?

Some of the obstacles arise from the nature of the U.S. foreign assistance program and others from inertia within a large bureaucracy and from ineffective sanctions against poor performance. Obstacles to change also come from the perception that flexibility will undermine congressional oversight and the ability to hold AID accountable for efficient use of funds, from insufficient demand by governments in developing countries, and from alleged misperceptions in AID and Congress about the nature of development management.

A major obstacle to change is the need in bureaucracies for well-defined operating procedures. Simon (1960) notes that organizations attempt to deal with routine, repetitive decisions through the application of models, standard operating procedures, and regulations that allow them to handle problems in a universal way and to maintain control over them. However, organizations must also deal with non-programmed decisions that are ill-structured, unique or uncertain and that require judgment, creativity, "rules of thumb," and heuristic problem solving. Sometimes the types of problems that an organization must deal with are misperceived to be programmable when, in reality, they are not. To a large extent, the development problems that AID must cope with are complex, uncertain, and unprogrammable. Its project cycle and procedures for designing, assessing, and implementing projects, however, are often programmed responses.

Part of the explanation for the intense criticism of AID is also found in different perceptions of the agency's functions. It was noted earlier that those who argue for stringent control often see the agency as an instrument of U.S. foreign and economic policy, while those who argue for more flexible and responsive management of projects see it primarily as an instrument for promoting social and economic development in poor countries. Often, the agency must respond to demands for greater control over its operations and its projects because the pressures to perform its political functions are stronger than those to perform its developmental ones.

The political nature of U.S. foreign aid is reflected in the fact that, although development assistance and economic support funds go to more than seventy countries, well over half is given to only nine countries in which the United States has strategic, military, or political interests. In 1984, for example, 62 percent of the nearly $4.5 billion allocated for development and economic support went to Egypt, Israel, Sudan, Pakistan, Turkey, Lebanon, Costa Rica, El Salvador, and Honduras. In that year, Egypt, Israel, Pakistan, and El Salvador alone received nearly half of the aid (McPherson, 1984).

Also, the belief that the transfer of technology and expertise is the primary means of promoting economic and social change is still pervasive in AID. And even if it were not, AID is politically obliged to show how foreign assistance benefits the U.S. economy. Thus about 70 percent of U.S. development assistance and economic support funds is now spent in the United States on purchases of U.S. goods and services.

Moreover, the argument that AID could not obtain funds from Congress if it claimed only to be experimenting, and unless it could show specifically what would be done and with what results, is a strong one in support of control-oriented management. The belief that AID must maintain an image of control and efficiency to obtain scarce funds from politically sensitive legislators for an agency that has a weak domestic constituency constrains the changes in procedures that its leaders are willing to advocate.

Merton (1940) long ago pointed out that when organizations must respond to strong demands for control, officials place strong emphasis on reliability in their procedures. This often leads to rigidity in behavior. Under such circumstances, only clearly defensible actions are taken within the organization even when more innovative, creative, and risky approaches may be needed. AID, like other bureaucracies, attempts to defend itself from criticism by instituting stronger controls over the allocation of funds, procurement, contracting, and management of projects.

Directions for Change in U.S. Foreign Aid

The review of experience with development administration presented in this book shows strong evidence that, if the U.S. foreign assistance program is truly concerned with improving the economic and social conditions of the poor in developing countries, it must begin to move toward more adaptive, responsive, and participatory approaches to planning and managing aid projects and programs.

The argument that such approaches are not yet operational is becoming less convincing as studies of more projects that were planned and managed in a participatory and collaborative manner with local organizations become available (Esman and Uphoff, 1984; Korten and Alfonso, 1982; Uphoff, 1986). Local action and learning process approaches have been used extensively and successfully for agricultural and rural development projects in Central America and Asia, and ironically, many were carried out by private or voluntary organizations funded by AID (Korten and Alfonso, 1982). Flexible and adaptive procedures have been used in carrying out rural water supply programs in Malawi, irrigation projects in Sri Lanka and the Philippines, and rural development projects in Bangladesh, Thailand, India, and other countries (Hafner and Rosenweign, 1984). In Latin America, a large number of projects have been implemented using participative action-learning approaches, and have often succeeded where large-scale government or international projects have had questionable results (Gran, 1983).

Nor is it clear that these methods are unsuited to large bureaucracies. The United Nations Children's Fund (UNICEF, 1982) has been using participative action-learning approaches in its "Urban Basic Services" projects in Sri Lanka, India, Peru, Indonesia, Mexico, Malaysia, Ethiopia, Ecuador, and several Central American countries, often with strong support from their governments. These projects are usually identified, plannned, and formulated collaboratively by community groups, government officials, and UNICEF advisors. Services are provided on a low-cost self-help basis, many project staff are selected by the community in which they work, and the activities are tailored to the conditions and needs of beneficiaries. The programs are planned and implemented concurrently.

In addition, studies of the Philippines' National Irrigation Administration showed that, with substantial training and bureaucratic reorientation, large government agencies can use action-learning and collaborative planning and management approaches effectively. The NIA has taken a strong role in assisting community irrigation groups to participate in planning and managing development activities (Korten and Carner, 1984).

AID officials' fear that Congress will not support such an approach to foreign assistance may also be overly pessimistic in light of the fact that Congress established in 1969, and continues to provide bipartisan support to, the Inter-American Foundation (IAF). This semiautonomous organization makes small grants to local private groups that help the poor improve their social and economic conditions (Bell, 1984). The IAF's trademark is experimentation. It supports a wide variety of self-help programs and projects, bypassing central governments and working directly with the poor. The beneficiaries themselves take the primary responsibility for project identification and design and for management and control of the projects' implementation. The IAF keeps its administrative costs low and works with a minimum of red tape—attempting to approve or reject project proposals within ninety days. It follows up with supervision and technical assistance in a low-key but effective way.

Clearly, the adoption of local action and learning process approaches to the administration of foreign assistance projects would require substantial adjustments within the AID bureaucracy. Korten and Uphoff (1981) point out that action learning requires changes in bureaucratic structure and in the attitudes and behavior of staff. But it also implies changes in job definitions, performance criteria, career incentives, planning and management procedures, and organizational responsibilities. The reorientation would result in the use of strategic management, flexible and simplified planning processes, responsive reward structures, flexible but long-term funding arrangements, and differentiated administrative units that give attention to the needs of different groups of clientele.

Although these changes are unlikely to come about quickly in the U.S. foreign aid program, one incremental means of moving in such a direction might be for AID to distinguish among, and attempt to plan and manage in different ways, projects and programs characterized by different degrees of uncertainty, ignorance, and risk. AID could also rely more heavily on nongovernmental and private voluntary organizations—which usually have a stronger record of using participative, collaborative, and flexible procedures successfully—to implement larger numbers of smaller assistance projects. The agency would also have to decentralize decision making and control more effectively to its field missions, whose staff would spend more time facilitating this process of interaction.

Real progress in reorienting the AID bureaucracy toward more flexible, adaptive, and responsive approaches to administration might also require giving less emphasis to projects as instruments of development and giving more attention to sectoral and program support. The Swedish International Development Agency (SIDA), for example, provides financial aid to a particular sector such as health, education, or agriculture without specifying in advance the activities or projects for which it will be used. This gives the recipients the options of allocating funds to those programs for which there is the greatest need or that have the greatest support, and to adjust their development activities quickly to changing needs and conditions.

Moreover, the successful adoption of more flexible and responsive administrative procedures might also require that the management of development and food assistance be completely separated from economic support funds and security assistance. Since most of the countries that the United States is attempting to influence are receiving large amounts of assistance in the form of security and economic support funds anyway, this approach would not really weaken U.S. leverage. In any case, little evidence supports the contention that development assistance, spread over a large number of countries in relatively small amounts as it now is, substantially influences whether or not governments in developing countries support U.S. foreign policy.

With the complete separation of development and security assistance, AID—as a development agency—could then be reorganized as a semiautonomous public corporation along the lines suggested by the Peterson committee in 1970 or along the lines of the Inter-American Foundation. This would give AID greater freedom to do what is necessary to promote economic and social improvements in the living conditions of the poor without being constrained by short-term foreign policy considerations. In this way, Congress could promote more flexible and responsive development assistance through AID, and still provide security assistance and economic support funds through a separate program to advance its foreign policy objectives without making aid a political weapon.

An Agenda for Future Research in Development Management

Whether or not AID accepts a "people-centered" philosophy of foreign assistance and development management, the agency will have to continue refining and retesting its current concepts and techniques of managment performance improvement and institutional development. Nearly all of its applied research indicates that there are still large gaps in knowledge about how to improve management performance in developing countries.

Among the most important research tasks are the following:

1. Refining the definitions of management performance and improvement and of institutional development in the wide range of cultural and political settings in which AID operates
2. Identifying the conditions under which management systems and control techniques are effective in improving project and program implementation and those under which local action, learning process, and "adaptive" forms of administration are more appropriate
3. Understanding better the role of informal processes of social interaction in development program and project implementation

4. Developing and testing appropriate research and evaluation methodologies and selecting appropriate "rules of evidence" for assessing the effectiveness of management approaches

5. Finding means of making the "learning process" approaches to management improvement more operational within the constraints in which AID must work

6. Assessing the effectiveness of institutional alternatives for implementing projects and programs in AID's high-priority sectors.

7. Applying more effectively the principles associated with "local action" and determining how to strengthen decentralized administrative arrangements in support of local action

8. Identifying and testing means of increasing bureaucratic responsiveness in institutions implementing AID projects in developing countries and of increasing AID's own capacity to respond more effectively to the wide range of conditions within which it must work in developing countries

Defining Management Improvement More Concisely

As the concept of development administration has changed in AID over the past thirty years, views of what institutions in developing countries should be doing to manage projects for economic and social development more effectively have also changed. The concept of management performance can be defined in many ways—as efficiency, effectiveness, responsiveness, or innovativeness—and can be measured by many different indicators. A danger often seen in the U.S. foreign aid program is the assumption that Western, "rationalistic" management techniques will improve performance in developing countries, ignoring the fact that management improvement may well be perceived, defined, and measured differently in other societies, cultures, and political systems. Thus far, AID staff and research contractors have used rather vague definitions of management performance improvement that may be so broad as to be meaningless, either for their own research or for formulating strategies of intervention in other societies and cultures.

More refined definitions of what management performance means can be generated from empirical and inductive studies of the countries in which AID is providing assistance and from among groups with different interests and perceptions within those countries. After more refined meanings of the terms are identified, measures or indicators must be developed that will allow AID and the organizations it assists to determine whether or not its interventions are in fact improving management performance.

Appropriateness of Different Approaches to Management Improvement

Additional research on the conditions under which management systems and control techniques are effective is also needed for improving project and program performance and those under which the learning process, local action, and "adaptive" forms of administration are more appropriate (Rondinelli, 1983).

The two strong streams of management intervention that are now being explored and used by AID—one that tends to rely heavily on improvement of management systems and controls, and the other that attempts to apply learning process and "adaptive" methods of organizational change—are not necessarily mutually exclusive, but they do differ in their underlying philosophies, basic assumptions, methods, techniques, and intended outcomes. AID's own project management system, which is reflected in the PBAR cycle and in AID's administrative procedures, is oriented toward the management systems and control process. As Herr (1982) has pointed out in his study of project management methodologies for DPMC, AID's approach to project management and those that it often prescribes in its training and technical assistance activities, tend to be top-down in orientation, focused primarily on the project as an instrument of development administration, concerned with the internal operations of individual projects, derived from "engineering" methods used primarily in physical infrastructure construction, and aimed largely at achieving efficiency.

Yet those who prescribe the local action, participatory, and learning process approaches question whether these assumptions and methods are the most useful in implementing programs effectively to achieve self-reliant and self-sustaining development. Montgomery (1980) makes a useful distinction between conditions under which management systems and controls can improve the delivery of routine services for the general public and those that require new and unconventional approaches to reach "special publics" and groups of the poor who are usually excluded from services needed to raise their incomes and standards of living. In general, public service delivery projects (those providing utilities, physical facilities, and infrastructure), management systems, and control techniques are more likely to be useful in improving management performance. The methods of analysis for decision making can be similar to those used for assessing the feasibility of economic investments. Engineering, technical, and economic expertise can be useful. The primary tasks of management are "to develop suitable routines for continuing service and impact." The organizational structures most appropriate for providing such services are government agencies and ministries, parastatal organizations, public corporations, and special authorities. Management performance can be evaluated by the organization's record in providing services at acceptable costs—that is, by efficiency criteria.

But projects aimed at providing social services such as health, education, and family planning—and at helping special groups that have been excluded from access to services because they live in peripheral areas or lack sufficient income to pay for them—must be managed by more flexible and adaptive means. Montgomery argues that numerous small-scale projects based on careful diagnoses of local needs and conditions are likely to be more effective than large-scale, general purpose projects. Implementing numerous small and carefully tailored programs and projects requires new and different approaches to management. Decisions cannot be made by investment criteria. They must be guided primarily by recurrent social analysis and feedback—what Korten calls a "learning process" and what Rondinelli (1983) terms "adaptive administration." The expertise of the social sciences is needed; the methods of diagnosis must be participative and interactive. The primary implementation task in these projects, Montgomery argues, is to "develop procedures for maximizing public use and responses." Management performance is measured by "progress in meeting changing special public needs."

Although government agencies are still required to play an important role, dealing effectively with special publics or groups of the poor with unique characteristics requires different procedures, attitudes, and behavior than is usually found in control-oriented bureaucracies. Special incentives must be given to administrators working in remote areas or among the poorest. The "cognitive distance" between government officials and the poor must be reduced through careful personnel recruitment and training. Moreover, paraprofessional staff, voluntary agencies, and organized special publics themselves may be more effective in reaching the poor than government bureaucracies. The most valuable function that government agencies can play in such situations is not to provide services directly, Montgomery contends, but to offer administrative resources in support of the work of more appropriate and effective organizations; that is, of extending their reach through unconventional means. Much of what AID has learned through its research into local action, integrated rural development, and learning processes can be used effectively to manage projects and programs of this kind.

However, an essential condition for using both the management control systems and the learning process methods that have already been developed in AID will be to identify more systematically the range of situations in which each can be effectively applied. Further research and field testing are needed to determine their uses and limitations in the wide variety of economic, social, and cultural settings in which AID works.

Understanding the Role of Informal Processes in Development Management

Much more research needs to be done on informal processes of social interaction in the planning and implementation of development programs.

Much of the attention of AID's contractors has been focused, since the mid-1970s, on building a case for learning process and local action as the preferred methods of institutional development. But little attention has been given to the processes and patterns of social interaction through which groups and organizations form the coalitions that allow action to be taken. Evaluations of development activities in a large number of developing countries indicate that informal processes of social and political interaction play a crucial role in the formulation of development policies, programs, and projects. Indeed, they may play a far greater role in influencing implementation than formal planning and management systems (Cleaves, 1974; Caiden and Wildavsky, 1974; Gordenker, 1976).

These and other studies also seem to indicate that many of the most successful administrators and institutions rely on various processes of informal and social interaction, either in place of or to supplement formal management processes (Grindle, 1977, 1980; Rondinelli, 1981; Bromley, 1981). They often use quite subtle and sophisticated methods of persuasion—information dissemination, public education, public relations, training, psychological field manipulation, and consultation and advisory processes—to influence other organizations in decision making. Studies have also shown the widespread use of what Lindblom (1965) calls methods of "mutual adjustment" such as tacit coordination, mediation of rewards and punishments, informal bargaining, negotiation, cooptation, coalition building, preemption, and authorititative prescription.

Lindblom (1965) suggests that processes of mutual adjustment are used most frequently (and are perhaps most valuable) under conditions in which it is politically difficult to define policy and program goals clearly, examine all alternatives exhaustively, identify socially optimal courses of action, and plan the implementation of policies and programs in detail. They are used most frequently when groups and organizations in a society have different goals, values, interests, or perceptions of the proper courses of action and when these differences cannot be reconciled simply through central control and coordination.

These are precisely the conditions that prevail in many countries where AID is funding development projects. Yet virtually no attention has been paid to these common forms of interaction through which managers and institutions pursue their interests. Consequently, little is known about how important these processes are in relation to formal management techniques in influencing management performance and institutional development or the degree to which they are used in conjunction with formal methods of management to implement projects and programs in developing countries. Clearly, indigenous informal methods of management will become more important if AID is successful in its goal of decentralizing decision making and administration in developing countries.

Applied research on this issue should attempt to identify and describe the processes of organizational interaction that have most frequently been used in AID project and program management, analyze the impacts of such processes on the effectiveness of project and program implementation, analyze the conditions under which social interaction processes can be used effectively either as substitutes for or as supplements to formal management techniques, and explore the implications for training administrators in methods of mutual adjustment in project management and program implementation.

Methods and Standards of Development Management Research

More attention must be given to developing appropriate applied research methods for the development administration research that AID sponsors and to identifying appropriate "rules of evidence" for determining the impacts of management assistance activities.

A debate has taken place within AID in recent years over the rigor of the applied research it has commissioned and the rules of evidence it has used to compare the outcomes of its development management assistance projects. The debate has often centered on the question of replicability—that is, whether the research and technical assistance are sufficiently well-structured and scientific enough to stand the scholarly test of replicability (two or more competent researchers being able to come up with the same results when observing the same phenomenon) on the one hand, and the pragmatic test of replicability (yielding results that allow widespread application of the project's results) on the other.

At one extreme, some critics argue that AID's applied research and field tests should be based on scientific methods such as those used in the physical sciences in which experimental and control groups are established to determine definitively the effects of management interventions. The objection to this argument is that AID rarely, if ever, funds projects that can be designed (and controlled sufficiently) to allow the impacts of interventions to be isolated and measured precisely. Strong arguments have been made recently that such research—or even rigorous social science variations of scientific methods—usually yield results that have had little or no influence on public policy making (Lindblom and Cohen, 1979; Wildavsky, 1979). It is more often the long accumulation of both "scientific" and "ordinary" knowledge, combined with the personal experience of those who participate in public policy making, that leads to changes in policy and action.

At the other extreme, some critics contend that scholarly standards of research and evidence are irrelevant to AID's needs; AID does not usually sponsor pure or original research. It most often sponsors "state-of-the-art" studies that review the findings of original research, and distill the implications for AID policy and technical assistance programs. Others contend that, if the local action and learning process approaches are indeed the most effective, each new development activity would be planned to meet the unique requirements of the intended target groups. Thus AID should not be concerned with replication in the conventional sense since it is unlikely that the conditions under which a project was successful would ever again be exactly the same. The objective of a learning process approach is not replication, but discovering how to tailor projects to the specific needs of different groups of people.

The methods of research and rules of evidence that are most likely to be useful to AID fall somewhere between these two extremes. AID has never shown much interest in "pure research"—USAID missions often complain that scholarly research is costly, time-consuming, abstract, and usually fails to address issues of immediate importance to them or to yield "action-oriented" policy and program implications. At the same time, even AID's most pragmatic field staff are unlikely to be convinced to adopt new methods and techniques of management improvement without some evidence that they will work.

AID must seek methods of applied research that both meet minimum standards of academic acceptability and provide guidelines for action. The challenge will be to promote an acceptable level of rigor in its applied research without inducing psuedoscientific rigor mortis.

Warwick's (1983) call for AID to adopt quantitative social science research methods comes close to those made during the 1960s for AID to adopt systems analysis for sector program research and project design. Attempts to apply systems analysis models or quantitative statistical techniques for research and evaluation in AID during the late 1960s met many difficulties and, a decade later, were strongly criticized within the agency. Evaluations indicate that agricultural and health sector analyses done by using systems models met severe difficulties in obtaining adequate and reliable data, and analysts often had to use inaccurate, unrealistic, or greatly simplified assumptions to fit the needs of the research designs; few of the USAID mission staffs or the policy makers in developing countries understood either the research methods or the significance of the findings. Moreover, the systems analyses were found to be costly and time-consuming. They had little real impact, except in a few unique cases, on influencing program and project management (Rice and Glaeser, 1972). If AID adopted the suggestions that it use rigorous social science methods, research funds could be shifted to the kinds of modeling and quantitative analyses that Lindblom and Cohen (1979) claim to have not been very useful in other Federal agencies.

Montgomery (1983: 295) correctly insists that arguments over "pure" and "applied" research are meaningless in AID. He suggests that research contracted by AID should be structured with a "decision-overlay" in which the following kinds of questions are asked: "Does a given element of knowledge or new insight contribute to improved policy? More precisely, what are the potential uses of a given research output in a specific context in which AID operates? How would the knowledge produced by a research contract (1) change a preference or style of operation of an individual or group whose behavior is relevant to AID's mission? or (2) reaffirm a doubtful or challenged preference or style of operation for such decision makers?"

Montgomery recommends that research be structured so that it is useful to the four major "actors" in AID activities: AID's Washington personnel, USAID mission staff, national government counterparts who receive U.S. assistance and are responsible for allocating resources to and supervising development programs, and project managers and their staff who are responsible for operating decisions.

The research contracted by AID for improving development management is most likely to be applied policy analysis. Although good policy analysis shares some of the same characteristics of more rigorous scientific research, the two differ in significant ways. Wildavsky (1979: 397-398) argues that the purpose of policy analysis is to help people understand and cope more effectively with their own problems through social interaction. As such, policy analysis is a craft and not a science. "Craft is distinguished from technique by the use of constraints to direct rather than deflect inquiry," he points out, "to liberate rather than imprison analysis within the confines of custom."

Good policy analysis, according to Wildavsky, compares alternative programs or courses of action by both their resources and objectives, and considers foregone opportunities. It focuses on outcomes and asks, "What does the distribution of resources look like, how should we evaluate it, and how should we change it to comport with our notions of efficiency and equity?" Good policy analysis, he contends, is tentative: "It suggests hypotheses that allow us to make better sense of our world." It promotes learning by "making errors easier to identify and by structuring incentives for their correction." Policy analysts must be skeptical and, therefore, use multiple and disaggregated verifying processes. Good policy analysis also "hedges its recommendations with margins of sensitivity to changes in underlying conditions." Finally, Wildavsky argues that good policy analysis examines problems in their historical contexts "so that error stands out ready for correction." Effective policy analysts remember people, "the professionals in the bureaus who must implement the programs, as well as the citizens whose participation in collective decision-making can either be enlarged or reduced by changes in the historical structure of social relationships." Policy analysis is most powerful and useful when it integrates the requirements of cognitive problem solving with those of social interaction. Thus this approach to policy analysis seems most appropriate for AID's development management research and evaluation activities.

Testing the Effectiveness of Alternative Organizations for Development Management

The effectiveness of alternative organizations and institutions for implementing development projects and programs in AID's priority sectors must also be analyzed and assessed. Research into organizational and institutional alternatives to the implementation of development activities by central government agencies also requires serious attention if AID is to implement successfully its management improvement strategies. In many developing countries, central bureaucracies are not the most effective organizations for implementing development projects aimed at promoting social change or alleviating poverty. Yet a large number of AID's institution-building projects have focused exclusively on central bureaucracies. A review (Barnett and Engel, 1982) of AID's portfolio of 659 institution-building projects that were implemented during the 1960s and 1970s found that 64 percent involved national ministries or agencies, and that the large majority of these provided assistance to national economic development and agriculture ministries and to central planning agencies. Only about one-third of the projects in the portfolio attempted to build the capcity of subnational and nongovernmental institutions.

As Moris (1984) has noted in a working paper for AID, much more must be known about the appropriateness of a wide variety of institutional and organizational arrangements, especially for promoting rural development. Many of AID's projects and programs have depended primarily on a national government ministry, a parastatal corporation, or a central rural development committee for implementation, many of which were neither effective nor appropriate. He suggests the need to explore a wide range of institutional alternatives including public corporations, educational institutions, multinational firms, indigenous enterprises, voluntary agencies, cooperative organizations, local administrative units, and government field agencies. Little systematic research has been done on determining the advantages and disadvantages of these institutions under different conditions and on developing criteria for making appropriate "institutional choices."

In order to apply effectively the principles of local action and responsive management, AID must also examine ways of decentralizing responsibility for the planning and implementation of development projects.

AID must identify the conditions that are necessary to create decentralized systems of administration that facilitate and support local action if that approach is to be used to develop administrative capacity. Research (Rondinelli, 1981, 1983; Cheema and Rondinelli, 1983; Rondinelli, Nellis and Cheema, 1983) indicates that developing countries have experimented with a variety of decentralization programs—deconcentration, delegation, devolution, and privatization—with mixed results. But the research on decentralization indicates that an essential factor in its success is the ability to create cooperative arrangements between central and local institutions and to reorient central bureaucracies from their traditional tasks of controlling and directing development programs to supporting and facilitating local action (Leonard, 1983). More research needs to be done by AID on ways of strengthening the "central-local interface" within the governments of developing countries.

Finally, means must be found and tested for increasing bureaucractic responsiveness to the needs of citizens in general, and the poor in particular, in planning and implementing development projects. AID's own project planning and management procedures must be made more flexible, and USAID missions must become more responsive to the social, economic, and physical needs of the intended beneficiaries before the agency can convince the governments receiving U.S. foreign aid that their bureaucracies should be more responsive to their citizens.

Development Administration as a Craft

In summary, although much has been learned since the inception of the U.S. foreign aid program in 1947 from research, technical assistance, and training about the effectiveness of alternative approaches to development administration and managment, much still remains to be learned. Economic and social development is still an uncertain, complex, and risky venture. The task of improving development administration must be approached, therefore, with realism, flexibility, and humility.

Perhaps the most important lesson that can be drawn from a review of AID's experience with trying to improve development administration is that, like Wildavsky's concept of policy analysis, *management too may be neither a science nor an art, but a craft.* Useful procedures, tools, and techniques can be taught and applied, but alone they no more allow a manager to achieve better administrative results than they enable a sculptor to carve a more beautiful statue or a cobbler to fashion a more comfortable pair of shoes. If management is really a craft, then tools and techniques are only effective if they are combined with skill, creativity, judgment, and experience. Although lessons of past experience can be useful in guiding action in the future, they must not be seen as universally applicable rules that invariably lead to success. The manager, like the craftsman, must know intimately the materials with which he or she works. A good craftsman must have access to the proper resources, operate in an environment in which his or her work is valued and rewarded, have the skill and imagination to use known methods and techniques appropriately and creatively, and have the experience and judgment to fashion new tools as the need arises. Some aspects of a craft can be improved with expert assistance and training. But lasting improvements in performance depend ultimately on the commitment, motivation, and perseverence of individual craftsmen.

References

Abbott, George C. (1973). "Two Concepts of Foreign Aid," World Development, Vol. 1, No. 9: 1-10.

Arkes, Hadley (1972). Bureaucracy, the Marshall Plan, and the National Interest, Princeton: Princeton University Press.

Ayubi, N. (1982). "Bureaucratic Inflation and Administrative Inefficiency: The Deadlock in Egyptian Administration," Middle Eastern Studies, Vol. 18, No. 1: 286-299.

Barnett, Stanley A. and Nat Engel (1982). Effective Institution Building, Washington: Office of Evaluation, U.S. Agency for International Development.

Beckington, Herbert (1983). "Testimony of AID Inspector General," United States Senate, Foreign Assistance and Related Programs and Appropriations, FY 1984, 98th Congress, 1st Session, Part 1, Hearings before the Committee on Appropriations (Committee Print), Washington: Government Printing Office.

Bell, Peter B. (1984). "Testimony of the Inter-American Fund President," U.S. Congress, House of Representatives, Foreign Assistance and Related Program Appropriations for 1984, Hearings Before a Subcommittee on Appropriations, 98th Congress, 1st Session, Washington: Government Printing Office: 81-111.

Bendor, Jonathan (1976). "A Theoretical Problem in Comparative Administration," Public Administration Review, Vol. 36, No. 6 (November/December): 626-631.

Birkhead, Guthrie S. (1967). "Institutionalization at a Modest Level: Public Administration Institute for Turkey and the Middle East," Syracuse, N.Y.: Syracuse University; mimeographed.

Blase, Hans C., and Luis A. Rodriguez (1968). "Introducing Innovation at Ecuadorian Universities," Pittsburgh, Pa.: Graduate School of Public and International Affairs, mimeographed.

Blase, Melvin G. (ed.) (1973). Institution Building: A Source Book,

Washington: U.S. Agency for International Development.

Brager, George, and Harry Specht (1973). Community Organizing, New York: Columbia University Press.

Bromley, Ray (1981). "From Cavalry to White Elephant: A Colombian Case of Urban Renewal and Marketing Reform," Development and Change, Vol. 12: 77-120.

Brown, David S. (1964). "The Key to Self-Help: Improving the Administrative Capabilities of Aid-receiving Countries," Public Administration Review, Vol. 24: 66-77.

Bryant, Coralie, Louise G. White, Elizabeth Shields, and Therese Borden (1983). "Research in Development Management: Learning About Effectiveness of Management Interventions," NASPAA Working Paper: Washington: National Association of Schools of Public Affairs and Administration.

Burke, W., and W. Schmidt (1971). "Management and Organizational Development," Personnel Management, Vol. 34.

Caiden, Naiomi, and Aaron Wildavsky (1974). Planning and Budgeting in Poor Countries, New York: John Wiley and Sons.

Cheema, G. Shabbir, and Dennis A. Rondinelli (eds) (1983). Decentralization and Development: Policy Implementation in Developing Countries, Beverly Hills: Sage.

Cleaves, Peter (1974). Bureaucrats, Politics and Administration in Chile, Berkeley: University of California Press.

Cohen, John M., Merilee S. Grindle, and John W. Thomas (1983). Knowledge-Building for Rural Development, Social Science and the Cooperative Agreements, Cambridge, Mass.: Harvard Institute for International Development.

Cohen, S.S., J. Dyckman, E. Schoenberger, and C.R. Downs (1981). Decentralization: A Framework for Policy Analysis, Berkeley: University of California, Institute for International Studies.

Conahan, Frank C. (1983). "Testimony of the Director of the International Division, General Accounting Office," United States Senate, Committee on Appropriations, Foreign Assistance and Related Programs, Appropriations for Fiscal Year 1983, Hearings, 97th Congress, 2nd Session, Washington: Government Printing Office.

Congressional Quarterly Service (1965). Congress and the Nation: Vol.I: 1945-1964, Washington: Congressional Quarterly Service.

Congressional Quarterly Service (1969). Congress and the Nation: Vol. II: 1965-1968, Washington: Congressional Quarterly Service.

Congressional Quarterly Service (1973). Congress and the Nation: Vol. III: 1969-1972, Washington: Congressional Quarterly Service.

Crawley, Roy W. (1965). "The Training of Public Servants," in M. Kriesberg (ed.) Public Administration in Developing Countries, Washington: The Brookings Institution: 162-176.

Eaton, Joseph W. (ed.) (1972). Institution Building and Development: From Concepts to Application, Beverly Hills: Sage Publications.

Edwards, Charles (1972). "Memorandum on Meeting with Ford Foundation Representatives on Development Administration Issues," Washington:

U.S. Agency for International Development; mimeographed.

Esman, Milton J. (1967). "The Institution-Building Concepts—An Interim Appraisal," Pittsburgh: Graduate School of Public and International Affairs, University of Pittsburgh.

Esman, Milton J. (1971). "CAG and the Study of Public Administration," in F.W. Riggs (ed.), Frontiers of Development Administration, Durham, N.C.: Duke University Press: 41-71.

Esman, Milton J. (1972). Administration and Development in Malaysia: Institution Building in a Plural Society, Ithaca, New York: Cornell University Press.

Esman, Milton J. (1980). "Development Assistance in Public Administration: Requiem or Renewal," Public Administration Review, Vol. 40, No. 5 (September/October): 426-431.

Esman, Milton J., and John D. Montgomery (1969)."Systems Approaches to Technical Cooperation: The Role of Development Administration," Public Administration Review, Vol. 29, No. 5: 507-538.

Esman, Milton J., and Norman T. Uphoff (1984). Local Organizations: Intermediaries in Rural Development, Ithaca, N.Y.: Cornell University Press.

Friedman, Milton (1958). "Foreign Economic Aid: Means and Objectives," in Gustav Ranis (ed.) The United States and the Developing Economies, New York: Norton: 250-263.

Gable, Richard W. (1975). Development Administration: Background, Terms, Concepts, Theories and a New Approach, Washington: U.S. Agency for International Development.

Gant, George F. (1966). "A Note on Applications of Development Administration," in John D. Montgomery and Arthur Smithies (eds.), Public Policy, Vol. XI, Cambridge, Mass.: Harvard University Graduate School of Public Administration: 199-211.

Gibson, James L., John M. Ivancevich, and James H. Donnelly, Jr.(1973). Organizations: Structure, Processes and Behavior, Dallas: Business Publications Inc.

Golembiewski, Robert T. (1969). "Organization Development in Public Agencies: Perspectives on Theory and Practice," Public Administration Review, Vol. 29 (July/August).

Golembiewski, R.T., C.W. Proehl, Jr., and D. Sink (1981). "Success of OD Applications in the Public Sector: Totting Up the Score for a Decade, More or Less," Public Administration Review, Vol. 41, No. 6 (November/December): 679-682.

Gordenker, Leon (1976). International Aid and National Decisions: Development Programs in Malawi, Tanzania and Zambia, Princeton: Princeton University Press.

Gran, Guy (1983). "Learning from Development Success: Some Lessons from Contemporary Case Histories," NASPAA Working Paper No. 9, Washington: National Association of Schools of Public Affairs and Administration.

Griffin, K.B., and J. Enos (1970). "Foreign Assistance: Objectives and Consequences," Economic Development and Cultural Change, Vol. l18: 313-327.

Grindle, Merilee S. (1977). Bureaucrats, Politicians and Peasants in Mexico, Berkeley: University of California Press.

Grindle, Merilee S. (ed.) (1980). Politics and Policy Implementation in the Third World, Princeton: Princeton University Press.

Hafner, Craig, and Fred Rosenweign (1984). "Water and Sanitation for Health Projects: Case Study: Malawi," paper presented at Workshop on Development Management, Annual Conference of the American Society of Public Administration.

Hanson, John W. (1968). Education, Nsukka: Study in Institution Building Among the Modern Ibo, East Lansing, Mich.: African Studies Center and Institute for International Studies in Education.

Herman, Chris, Margaret Shaw, and John Hannah (1985). The Management Impact of Liberia's Agricultural Sector Analysis and Planning Project and the Agricultural Development Program, Washington: U.S. Agency for International Development.

Herr, Robert J. (1982). Project Analysis: Toward An Integrated Methodology, Washington: Development Project Management Center, U.S. Department of Agriculture.

Hirschman, Albert O. (1959). The Strategy of Economic Development, New Haven: Yale University Press.

Holdcroft, Lane E. (1978). The Rise and Fall of Community Development in Developing Countries, 1950-1965: A Critical Analysis and an Annotated Bibliography, AID Contract/ta-CA-3; Washington: Office of Rural Development and Development Administration, U.S. Agency for International Development.

Honadle, G., E. Morss, J. VanSant, and D. Gow (1980). Integrated Rural Development: Making it Work?, Washington: Development Alternatives Inc.

Huntington, Samuel P. (1971). "The Change to Change," Comparative Politics, Vol. 3 (April): 283-322.

Ilchman, Warren F. (1971). "Comparative Public Administration and Conventional Wisdom," Comparative Politics Series Vol. 2, Beverly Hills, California: Sage Publications.

Ingle, Marcus D. (1970). "Current Village Administration, 1970," Saigon, Vietnam: U.S. Agency for International Development.

Ingle, Marcus D. (1979). Implementing Development Programs: A State of the Art Review, Washington: U.S. Agency for International Development.

Ingle, Marcus D., and E. Edward Rizzo (1981). "A Performance Improvement Approach," Washington: Development Project Management Center, U.S. Department of Agriculture.

Ingle, Marcus D., Dennis A. Rondinelli, and Thyra Riley (1981). Managing Benefits for the Poor: Approaches, Experience, and Strategies for Improvement, Washington: U.S. Agency for International Development.

Ingle, Marcus D., Morris J. Solomon, Pierrette J. Countryman, and Merlyn H. Kettering (1981). "Promising Approaches to Project Management Improvement," Washington: Development Project Management Center, U.S. Department of Agriculture.

Jackson, Sir Robert (1969). A Study of the Capacity of the United Nations System, Geneva: United Nations.

Kettering, Merlyn H. (1980). "Action Training in Project Planning and Management: A Review of the Experience of the National Planning Project of USAID-Government of Jamaica 1976-1979," Working Paper, Washington: Development Project Management Center, U.S. Department of Agriculture.

Kettering, Merlyn H., and Terry D. Schmidt (1981). Improving Project Monitoring and Implementation Systems: A Strategy and Implementation Plan for a Project Management Information System for USAID/Thailand, Washington: Development Project Management Center, U.S. Department of Agriculture.

Korten, David C. (1980). "Community Organization and Rural Development: A Learning Process Approach," Public Administration Review, Vol. 40, No. 5: 480-511.

Korten, David C. (1981). "Management of Social Transformation," Public Administration Review, Vol. 41, No. 6 (November/December): 609-618.

Korten, David C. (1982). "The Working Group as a Mechanism for Managing Bureaucratic Reorientation: Experience From the Philippines," NASPAA Working Paper No. 4, Washington: National Association of Schools of Public Affairs and Administration.

Korten, David C. (1983). "Learning From USAID Field Experience: Institutional Development and the Dynamics of the Project Process," NASPAA Working Paper No. 7, Washington: National Association of Schools of Public Affairs and Administration.

Korten, David C., and Norman T. Uphoff (1981). "Bureaucratic Reorientation for Participatory Rural Development," Working Paper No. 1, Washington: National Association of Schools of Public Affiars and Administration.

Korten, David C., and Felipe B. Alfonso (eds.) (1982). Bureaucracy and the Poor: Closing the Gap, West Hartford, Conn: Kumarian Press.

Korten, David C., and George Carner (1984), "Reorienting Bureaucracies to Serve People: Two Experiences in the Philippines," Canadian Journal of Development Studies, Vol. V, No. 1 (1984): 7-24.

Koteen, Jack, Edward Rizzo, David Jickling, and Kenneth Kornher (1970). "Key Problems in Development Administration," Washington: U.S. Agency for International Development; mimeographed.

Kramer, Ralph M., and Harry Specht (eds.) (1975). Readings in Community Organization Practice, 2nd Edition, Englewood Cliffs: Prentice Hall.

Kuznets, Simon (1966). Modern Economic Growth, New Haven: Yale University Press.

Landau, Martin (1970). "Development Administration and Decision Theory," in E. Weidner (ed.) Development Administration in Asia, Durham, N.C.: Duke University Press, 73-103.

Lee, Hahn-Been (1970). "The Role of the Higher Civil Service Under Rapid Social and Economic Change," in E. Weidner (ed.) Development Administration in Asia, Durham, N.C.: Duke University Press, 107-131.

Leonard, David K. (1982). "Analyzing the Organizational Requirements for Serving the Rural Poor," in D.K. Leonard and D.R. Marshall (eds.), Institutions of Rural Development for the Poor: Decentralization and Organizational Linkages, Berkeley: University of California, Institute for International Studies: 1-39.

Leonard, David K. (1983). "Interorganizational Linkages for Decentralized Rural Development: Overcoming Administrative Weaknesses," in G.S. Cheema and D.A. Rondinelli (eds), Decentralization and Development: Policy Implementation in Developing Countries, Beverly Hills: Sage: 271-294.

Leonard, David K. (1984). "The Political Realities of African Management," Paper Prepared for Workshop in Preparation for the Development Management and Impact Evaluation Series, Washington: U.S. Agency for International Development.

Levinson, J., and J. deOnis (1970). The Alliance That Lost Its Way: A Critical Report on the Alliance for Progress, Chicago: Quadrangle.

Lindblom, Charles E. (1965). The Intelligence of Democracy: Decision-Making Through Mutual Adjustment, New York: The Free Press.

Lindblom, Charles E., and David K. Cohen (1979). Useable Knowledge: Social Science and Social Problem Solving, New Haven: Yale University Press.

Loveman, Brian (1976). "The Comparative Administration Group, Development Administration and Antidevelopment," Public Administration Review, Vol. 36, No. 6: 616-621.

McPherson, Peter (1984). "Testimony of the AID Administrator," U.S. Congress, House of Representatives, Foreign Assistance and Related Program Appropriations for 1984, Hearings Before a Subcommittee on Appropriations, 98th Congress, 1st Session, Washington: Government Printing Office: 122-125.

Merton, Robert K. (1940). "Bureaucratic Structure and Personality," Social Forces, No. 18: 560-568.

Montgomery, John D. (1980). "Administering to the Poor (Or, If We Can't Help Rich Dictators, What Can We Do for the Poor?" Public Administration Review, Vol. 40, No. 5 (September/October): 421-425.

Montgomery, John D. (1983). "Improving the Utility of AID-Sponsored Research," Working Paper, Cambridge, Mass: Harvard Institute of International Development.

Montgomery, John D., Rufus B. Hughes, and Raymond H. Davis (1964). "Rural Improvement and Political Development: The JCRR Model," Washington: U.S. Agency for International Development.

Moris, Jon R. (1981). Managing Induced Rural Development, Bloomington: PASITAM, Indiana University Institute for International Development.

Moris, Jon R. (1984). "Institutional Choice for Rural Development," Working Paper, Cambridge: Harvard Institute of International Development.

Morss, E.R., J.K. Hatch, D.R. Mickelwait, and C.F. Sweet (1975). Strategies for Small Farmer Development: An Empirical Study of Rural Development Projects, Vols. I and II, Washington: Development Alternatives Incorporated.

Morton, Alice L. (1978). "Briefing Paper on Local Action Guidance and Implementation," Washington: USAID, Rural and Development Administration Office; mimeographed.

Morton, Alice L. (1979). "Project Evaluation—Local Action Guidance and Implementation" AID/CM/ta-C-73-41, Washington: U.S. Agency for International Development, mimeographed.

Nicholson, Norman K., Donald Bowles, Ndungu Gathinji, and Elinor Ostrom (1985). Egerton College Impact Evaluation Report, Washington: U.S. Agency for International Development.

Owens, Edgar, and Robert d'A. Shaw (1972). Development Reconsidered, Lexington, Mass.: D.C. Heath.

Painter, Thomas M. with Roger Poulen, David Harmon and Douglas Barnett (1985). Development Management in Africa: The Case of the Niamey Department Development Project, Niger Republic, Washington: U.S. Agency for International Development.

Paul, Samuel (1983). "Training for Public Administration and Management in Developing Countries: A Review," World Bank Staff Working Paper 584, Washington: World Bank.

Pearson, Lester (1969). Partners in Development, New York: Praeger Publishers.

Pyle, David F. (1982). "From Project to Program: Structural Constraints Associated with Expansion," NASPAA Working Paper No. 3, Washington: National Association of Schools of Public Affairs and Administration.

Ralston, Lenore, James Anderson, and Elizabeth Colson (1983). Voluntary Efforts in Decentralized Management: Opportunities and Constraints in Rural Development, Berkeley: University of California, Institute for International Studies.

Rice, E.B., and E. Glaeser (1972). "Agricultural Sector Studies: An Evaluation of AID's Recent Experience," AID Evaluation Papers, No 5, Washington: U. S. Agency for International Development.

Riggs, Fred W. (1970). Administrative Reform and Political Responsibility: A Theory of Dynamic Balancing, Sage Professional Papers in Comparative Politics, Vol. I, Beverly Hills, Calif: Sage Publications.

Riggs, Fred W. (1971). "The Context of Development Administration," in F. Riggs (ed.) Frontiers of Development Administration, Durham, N.C.: Duke University Press: 72-108.

Riggs, Fred W. (1971a). "Introduction," in F.W. Riggs (ed.) Frontiers of Development Administration, Durham, N.C.: Duke University Press: 3-37.

Rizzo, E. Edward, and Jack Koteen (1976). "Guidelines for Appraisal of Recipient's Project Management Capacity," Washington: U.S. Agency for International Development, Office of Development Administration; mimeographed.

Rizzo, E. Edward, Alfred Davidson, and Monteze Snyder (1980). "A.I.D. Strategies for Health Management Improvement," Washington: USAID, Office of Development Administration; mimeographed.

Rondinelli, Dennis A. (1971). "Community Development and American Pacification Policy in Vietnam," Philippine Journal of Public Administration, Vol. XV, No. 2: 162-174.

Rondinelli, Dennis A. (1976). "International Requirements for Project Planning: Aids or Obstacles to Development Planning?" Journal of the American Institute of Planners, Vol. 43, No. 3: 314-326.

Rondinelli, Dennis A. (1976a). "Why Development Projects Fail: Problems of Project Management in Developing Countries," Project Management Quarterly, Vol. VII, No. 1: 10-15.

Rondinelli, Dennis A. (1976b). "International Assistance Policy and Development Project Administration: The Impact of Imperious Rationality," International Organization, Vol. 30, No. 4: 573-605.

Rondinelli, Dennis A. (ed.), (1977). Planning Development Projects, Stroudsburg, Pa.: Hutchinson and Ross Publishing Company.

Rondinelli, Dennis A. (1979). "Planning Development Projects: Lessons From Developing Countries," Long Range Planning, Vol. 12, No. 3: 48-56.

Rondinelli, Dennis A. (1981). "Administrative Decentralization and Economic Development: Sudan's Experiment with Devolution," Journal of Modern African Studies, Vol. 19, No. 4:595-624.

Rondinelli, Dennis A. (1982). "The Dilemma of Development Administration: Uncertainty and Complexity in Control-Oriented Bureaucracies," World Politics, Vol. 35, No. 1: 43-72.

Rondinelli, Dennis A. (1983). Development Projects as Policy Experiments: An Adaptive Approach to Development Administration, New York and London: Methuen and Company.

Rondinelli, Dennis A. (1984). "Development Administration," in Adam Kuper and Jessica Kuper (eds.), The Social Science Encyclopaedia, London: Routledge and Kegan Paul: 195-196.

Rondinelli, Dennis A. (1986). Practical Lessons for Development Management: Experience with Implementing Agricultural Development Projects in Africa, AID Evaluation Special Study, Washington: U.S. Agency for International Development.

Rondinelli, Dennis A., and H. Raymond Radosevich (1974). An Integrated Approach to Development Project Management, Report to the U.S. Agency for International Development on Modernizing Management for Development, Washington: U. S. Agency for Internatinal Development.

Rondinelli, Dennis A., John R. Nellis and G. Shabbir Cheema (1983). "Decentralization in Developing Countries: A Review of Recent Experience," World Bank Staff Working Paper No. 581, Washington: World Bank.

Rosenthal, Irving, Leroy Jackson, Ruth Mara, and Laura McPherson (1985). Development Management in Africa: The Case of the North Shaba Rural Development Project in Zaire, Washington: U.S. Agency for International Development.

Rostow, Walt W. (1952). The Process of Economic Growth, New York: Norton.

Sanders, Irwin T. (1958). Community Development and National Change, Summary of Conference on Community Development at the Massachusetts Institute of Technology; Washington: U.S. International Cooperation Agency.

Selim, Hassan M. (1983). Development Assistance Policies and the Performance of Aid Agencies, New York: St. Martin's Press.

Seymour, Matt, Laura McPherson, and David Harmon (1985). Development Management in Africa: The Case of the Bakel Small Irrigated Perimeters Project in Senegal, Washington: U.S. Agency for International

Development.

Siffin, William J. (1967). "The Thai Institute of Public Administration: A Case Study in Institution Building," Pittsburgh, Pa.: University of Pittsburgh; mimeographed.

Siffin, William J. (1976). "Two Decades of Public Administration in Developing Countries," Public Administration Review, Vol. 36, No. 1 (January/February): 61-71.

Sigelman, Lee (1976). "In Search of Comparative Administration," Public Administration Review, Vol. 36, No. 6 (November/December): 621-625.

Simon, Herbert A. (1960). The New Science of Management Decision, New York: Harper and Row.

Smart, Lyman F. (ed.) (1970). Proceedings of the Regional Conference on Institution Building, Conference sponsored by the U.S. Agency for International Development, Logan, Utah: Utah State University.

Solomon, Morris (1974). "A Program for Achieving Better Project Management in Development Countries," Washington: USAID and Vanderbilt University Graduate School of Management; mimeographed.

Solomon, Morris (1983). "The Action Training Workshop as a Tool for Financial and Program Management Improvement," Washington: U.S. Department of Agriculture, Development Project Management Center.

Solomon, M., M. Kettering, P. Countryman, and M. Ingle (1981). "Promising Approaches to Project Management Improvement," Washington: U.S. Department of Agriculture, Development Project Management Center.

Spengler, Joseph (1963). "Bureaucracy and Economic Development," in J. LaPalombara (ed.) Bureaucracy and Political Development, Princeton: Princeton University Press, 199-232.

Stout, Russell, Jr. (1980). Management or Control? The Organizational Challenge, Bloomington: Indiana University Press.

Taylor, Carl (1984). "Testimony for the American Health Association," U.S. Congress, House of Representatives, Foreign Assistance and Related Program Appropriations for 1984, Hearings Before a Subcommittee on Appropriations, 98th Congress, 1st Session, Washington: Government Printing Office.

Tendler, Judith (1975). Inside Foreign Aid, Baltimore: Johns Hopkins University Press.

Thomas, Theodore (1983). "Reorienting Bureaucratic Performance: A Social Learning Approach to Development Action," NASPAA Working Paper No. 8, Washington: National Association of Schools of Public Affairs and Administration.

Thompson, Victor A. (1964). "Administrative Objectives for Development Administration," Administrative Science Quarterly, Vol. 9 (June): 91-108.

Thorp, Willard T. (1951). "Some Basic Policy Issues in Economic Development," American Economic Review, Vol. XLI, No. 2: 407-417.

Tumin, Melvin M. (1958). "Some Social Requirements for Effective Community Development," Community Development Review, No. 11 (December): 1-39.

Tuthill, Jane (1985). "Signposts in Development Management: A Computer-based Analysis of 277 Projects in Africa" Washington: U.S. Agency for International Development.

United Nations Children's Fund (UNICEF) (1982). Urban Basic Services: Reaching Children and Women of the Urban Poor, Report by the Executive Director, New York: United Nations Economic and Social Council, 1982. Doc. No. E/ICEF/L.1440.

Uphoff, Norman T. (1986). Local Institutional Development, West Hartford, Conn: Kumarian Press.

Uphoff, Norman T., John M. Cohen and Arthur A. Goldsmith (1979). Feasibility and Application of Rural Development Participation, Monograph Series No. 3, Ithaca, N.Y.: Cornell University, Rural Development Committee.

Uphoff, Norman T., and Milton J. Esman (1974). Local Organizations for Rural Development: Analysis of the Asian Experience, Ithaca, N.Y.: Cornell University Center for International Studies.

U.S. Agency for International Development (1973). "Interregional Programs in Development Administration," Washington: USAID Office of Development Administration; mimeographed.

U.S. Agency for International Development (1975). Project Management: Project Paper, Project No. 931-11-O96, Washington: USAID, Office of Development Adminstration; mimeographed.

U.S. Agency for International Development (1975a). Report of the AID Work Group on Management Improvement and Development Administration, Washington: USAID; mimeographed.

U.S. Agency for International Development (1975b). Implementation of the "New Directions" in Development Assistance, Report to the Committee on International Relations on Implementation of Legislative Reforms in the Foreign Assistance Act of 1973; U.S. House of Representatives, 94th Congress, 1st Session, (Committee Print).

U.S. Agency for International Development (1977). "Policy Determination—Development Administration," PD-69, AID Handbook, Vol. 2, Sup. B6.

U.S. Agency for International Development (1978). "Administration and Organization of Integrated Rural Development: Project Paper," Washington: USAID Office of Rural and Administrative Development; mimeographed.

U.S. Agency for International Development (1979). Managing Decentralization Project Paper, Washington: USAID.

U.S. Agency for International Development (1980). Country Development Strategy Statement—Kenya, Washington: USAID.

U.S. Agency for International Development (1980a). Country Development Strategy Statement—Costa Rica, Washington: USAID.

U.S. Agency for International Development (1980b). Country Development Strategy Statement—Bangladesh, Washington: USAID.

U.S. Agency for International Development (1980c). Country Development Strategy Statement—Philippines, Washington: USAID.

U.S. Agency for International Development (1982). Development Administration Strategy Paper, Washington: USAID.

U.S. Agency for International Development (1982a). Evaluation of the Project Management Effectiveness Project, Washingtion: USAID.

U.S. Agency for International Development (1982b). Performance Management Project Paper, Washington: USAID.

U.S. Agency for International Development (1983). Annual Budget Submission to the Congress, Washington: USAID.

U.S. Agency for International Development (1983a). Semiannual Report of the Inspector General As of September 30, 1983, Washington: USAID.

U.S. Agency for International Development (1985). Blueprint for Development: The Strategic Plan of the Agency for International Development, Washington: USAID.

U.S. Code Congressional and Administrative News (1973). Vol. 2, St. Paul, Minn: West Publishing Company.

U.S. Congress, Senate Foreign Relations Committee (1973). Foreign Assistance Act of 1973: Report of the Committee on Foreign Relations, United States Senate on S. 2335, 92nd Congress, 1st Session, Report No. 93-377, Washington: Government Printing Office.

U.S. General Accounting Office (1985). Limited Sahelian Government Capabilities to Administer Economic Assistance Affects their Economic Development, Report No. 472037, Washington: Government Printing Office.

U.S. General Accounting Office (1982). Experience—A Potential Tool for Improving U.S. Assistance Abroad, Report No. GAO/ID-82-36, Washington: Government Printing Office.

U.S. General Accounting Office (1983). Donor Approaches to Development Assistance: Implications for the United States, Report GAO/ID-83-23, Washington: Government Printing Office.

U.S. General Accounting Office (1985). Limited Sahelian Government Capabilities to Administer Economic Assistance Affects their Economic Development, Report No. 472037,Washington: Government Printing Office.

Warren, Marion, George Honadle, Sam Montsi, and Bob Walter (1985). Development Management in Africa: The Case of the Land Conservation and Range Development Program in Lesotho, Washington: U.S. Agency for International Development.

Warwick, Donald P. (1983). "Improving Research Methodology," Working Paper, Cambridge, Mass.: Harvard Institute of International Development.

Waterston, Albert (1965). Development Planning: Lessons of Experience, Baltimore: The Johns Hopkins University Press.

Waterston, Albert (1973). "The Agricultural Sector Implementation Project," Washington: Governmental Affairs Institute; mimeographed.

Waterston, Albert, Wayne Weiss, and John L. Wilson (1976). Managing Planned Agricultural Development, AID Contract No. AID/csd-3630, Washington: Governmental Affairs Institute.

Weidner, Edward W. (1964). Technical Assistance in Public Administration Overseas: The Case for Development Administration, Chicago: Public

Administration Service.

Wildavsky, Aaron (1979). Speaking Truth to Power: The Art and Craft of Policy Analysis, Boston: Little Brown.

Wolf, Charles (1960). Foreign Aid: Theory and Practice in Southern Asia), Princeton: Princeton University Press.

World Bank (1983). World Development Report 1983. Washington: World Bank.

Xuan, Nguyen-Duy (1970). "Technical Assistance to a Public Administration Institute: The Vietnam Case," in E.W. Weidner (ed.), Development Administration in Asia, Durham, N.C.: Duke University Press: 366-398.

Afterword

Dennis Rondinelli has written an authoritative and well documented book on development administration in the U.S. foreign aid program. As an advisor to AID's public administration programs during the 1960s and as a scholar with a continuing interest in comparative and development administration, my reflections focus on the political implications of AID's experience with development administration, and on ways in which AID can improve its own capacity to manage development assistance programs more effectively in the future.

Rondinelli concludes that although AID has sponsored a great deal of research on development administration and tried many approaches to strengthening administration in developing countries, there remains a large gap between the knowledge generated from research and experience and the way the agency actually operates. It seems that AID has not been able to bring about fundamental administrative reforms either in developing countries or in its own operations.

The gap between knowledge and action in AID's development administration activities can be fully explained only by examining underlying political factors. In Chapter 1, Rondinelli identifies the constituencies affecting AID policies and reveals one of the most important reasons for many of its failings: most of those constituencies are domestic. Groups in the host countries who influence AID policies are "counterpart officials," and citizens and their representatives usually do not participate.

To the degree that public officials in many Third World countries are a kind of "ruling class," simply because of the absence or weakness of representative institutions for self- government, they are free to manage public affairs in their own interests. No doubt they often see foreign aid as a way of gaining fringe benefits for themselves, even though few advantages "trickle down" to the general public, and especially to the poor. Without changing the distribution of power in host countries, of course, it is hard to see how things could be otherwise. It is not normally in the interest of the public officials (military or civil) who channel U.S. AID projects to bring about fundamental political changes. Rondinelli states the facts plainly enough, but it would shed some light on the reasons for AID's difficulties to point out that the political and technical priorities of AID have not, for structural reasons, been influenced directly by the interests of non-governmental constituencies in the recipient countries. By contrast, the best administered domestic programs in U.S. public administration typically, I believe, involve rather direct accountability of officials to their public constituents.

Rondinelli points out correctly that AID was not influenced strongly by the Comparative Administration Group's work on political development. But I disagree that it was because "CAG's work remained somewhat abstract." I think that AID could not accept the political analysis offered in many CAG papers. The reasons for this become apparent when one understands more about the basic political context of AID itself—being unaccountable to its ultimate clientele, the people of the aided countries, and about the background of its staff members—most AID staff understood quite well how to be good administrators in the U.S., but they were not prepared by experience or training to understand the political requisites of administrative development in Third World countries.

The basic weakness of AID's approach to improving public administration has been, in my opinion, its fixation on economic growth as a goal without any genuine understanding of the political prerequisites of effective administration, to say nothing of having well defined political development goals. It remained for Congress to insert Title IX into the Foreign Assistance Act during the late 1960s. The goal of the congressional liberals who sponsored this legislation was clearly to promote "democratization." But they were not able to win majority support in Congress. Thus, they compromised by accepting a weak and vague injunction to assure "maximum participation in the task of economic development" by the people of developing countries, especially through "democratic local government institutions." A Title IX office was established in AID to work with all the program departments for implementation of the participation goal. My impression, however, is that AID staff members largely ignored Title IX, viewing it as a congressional whim rather than as a serious basis for action.

The growing disparity between rich and poor, pointed to by Owens and Shaw in the early 1970s, quite properly drew attention to one of the main weaknesses of the economic growth orientation. The rhetoric about "new directions" and "new realities" in the 1973 legislation seems to mask insensitivity to the political structures—international as well as domestic—that undergird the privileges of the rich and the poverty of the oppressed. I cannot help but agree with Senator Fulbright's criticisms, reported by Rondinelli in Chapter 4. So long as AID's programs are channeled through government bureaucracies, they can scarcely avoid the kinds of manipulation that prevent serious challenge to the status quo.

To reinforce the dedication to public service of government officials it is necessary to strengthen extra-bureaucratic political institutions; otherwise bureaucratic accountability remains weak. Politics and administration, despite the myth of separation, are in fact inextricably intertwined, perhaps even more so in developing countries than in the United States. Efforts to develop administration that fail to take the political context of public bureaucracies into account will surely fail.

If AID has failed to learn from its own evaluative studies, as Rondinelli argues, we may conclude that there is a need to supplement the overseas focus by taking a closer look at the dynamics of program administration within AID. Resistance to learning from research within AID cannot be overcome just by giving more information and preparing more reports by consultants. As Rondinelli emphasizes, "the degree to which AID can refine and apply the findings of development administration studies will depend on the degree to which the philosophies underlying them can be made more widely acceptable within AID, Congress and the Executive Branch (146-147)."

When it prepares testimony for legislative hearings, AID could involve some people who can speak from first-hand experience about the impact of our foreign assistance programs on "target groups." This would serve AID's objectives by making its work more credible to congressmen. If they are persuaded of the validity of the "adaptive learning, local action, and assisted self-help" approaches, they would be able at the political level to strengthen the efforts of those within AID who are already committed to this philosophy.

AID could also make better use of external resources— university specialists with overseas experience, Third World scholars working in the United States, the staff of foundations funding development activities, consultants, and the staff of overseas development institutions—to give Congress a better understanding of the complexities of and opportunities for improving the management of AID programs.

AID also needs to disseminate the findings of research under-taken in the area studies programs of U.S. universities to its staff. My impression is that over and over again we have reinvented the wheel, we have rediscovered things that were once well known but sub-sequently forgotten. Surely the development of institutional memories, both in developing countries and in AID itself, is an impor-tant facet of development administration. AID cannot develop appro-priate technologies or really understand local conditions without making good use of a mass of basic research already available in the area studies literature, and in research done on comparative adminis-tration and comparative politics. A model might be found in the State Department, which for a long time has had a section for External Re-search. It monitors the studies of university scholars that are judged to be relevant to the foreign relations concerns of the department.

Only by recognizing the inextricable relationships between poli-tics and administration, and by closing the gap between knowledge and action, can AID hope to improve its own management and to as-sist public and private organizations in developing countries to strengthen their administrative capacity.

Fred W. Riggs

Index